Reader's Theater...
and So Much More!

Written by: Brenda McGee and Tom McGee
Cover Art and Illustrations by: Brandon Bolt
Edited by: Debbie Keiser and Linda Triska

ISBN 978-1-59363-241-0
© 2008 Prufrock Press Inc.

Table of Contents

Overview:

Reader's Theater is a thinking, reading, writing, speaking, and listening experience. Readers should rely on their vocal abilities to portray a character. Students should strive for voice flexibility, crisp articulation, proper pronunciation, and projection.

These plays and skits are not meant to be staged performances. There is no need for sets, elaborate props, or costumes. However, it might be fun to add more drama with minimal stage direction and easy-to-find props.

If you decide you would like to make one or more of the Reader's Theaters into major productions, it is suggested that students work in committees and divide the responsibilities for creating a live performance. This would involve everything from designing scenery to writing invitations and programs. This could also be an economics lesson using budgets and selling concessions.

These Reader's Theaters were written for all students to enjoy as they develop their sense of humor, improve oral communication, knowledge of content, fluency, comprehension, self-confidence, and boost interest in reading.

Management:

Scan the plays and assign parts you believe would fit a student's comfort level based on reading ability.

Give students an opportunity to read their parts silently and ask questions about any unfamiliar words. The objective is fluency and oral expression, not cold reading.

If there are too many characters, assign students with smaller parts more than one character.

If you have too few parts, cut some of the longer parts into more than one part. Another idea would be to challenge students as a class, or small group, to create more characters and add more parts.

Even the most reluctant and shy students enjoy Reader's Theaters. This is "learning can be fun" at its best!

Reader's Theater Skills

Sight-Word Reading
- reads numerous high-frequency words fluently

Vocabulary Development
- learns new vocabulary by listening, reading, or instruction

Comprehending What Is Read
- uses context clues to determine word meanings
- predicts and verifies outcomes
- recognizes and analyzes characters, setting, and plot in a passage listened to or read
- makes and explains inferences and supports with evidence from text
- identifies facts and details
- identifies the explicit and implicit main idea of a passage
- draws conclusions and supports with text evidence

Literary Response
- retells a story without a book, including beginning, middle, and end
- retells a story including important events and details
- summarizes or paraphrases text
- identifies through retelling or acting out the correct sequence of events in a story

Oral Communication
- speaks to an audience using appropriate volume and rate
- adapts oral language to purpose, audience, and occasion
- presents dramatic interpretations
- presents for an audience

Listening Skills
- listens actively and purposefully
- listens, enjoys, and appreciates spoken language

Humor Terms in Literature

exaggeration - to make something greater than it actually is; to stretch or magnify the truth

farce - an exaggerated comedy based on broadly humorous situations; play intended only to be funny; absurd or ridiculous

figure of speech - any phrase or saying that is not meant to be taken literally; this includes idioms, hyperboles, etc.

hyperbole – an exaggeration in writing used to make a point

idiom – a phrase that means one thing word for word (or literally) but suggests a different meaning

irony – when you expect one thing to happen, but then the opposite happens

parody – literary or artistic work that imitates the characteristic style of an author, or a work for comic effect or ridicule

pun – the humorous use of a word, or of words, which are formed or sound alike but have different meanings, in such a way as to play on two or more of the possible applications; a play on words

sarcasm – a taunting, sneering, cutting, or caustic remark; gibe or jeer, generally ironical

satire – manner of writing that mixes a critical attitude with wit and humor in an effort to improve mankind and human institutions

understatement – expressing an idea with less emphasis or in a lesser degree than is the actual case; the opposite of hyperbole. Understatement is used for ironic emphasis.

Notes

Act 1

Reader's Theaters

Pre-Reading Suggestions:

Prediction

Have students discuss what a play entitled "Waiting Room" could be about. Record responses on the board.

Point of View

Tell students this play is written with an unusual point of view (way of telling a story). Ask: What different ways (points of view) do you think you could write a play entitled "Waiting Room?"

Assessing Prior Knowledge

Explain that this play takes place in a veterinarian's waiting room. Ask students to brainstorm the kinds of animals that might be seen in a veterinarian's office and the kinds of care that might be provided.

Post-Reading Suggestions –

Expressing Ideas in Writing

•   Have students work in small groups to rewrite the ending to the play. Encourage them to share with the group.

•   Challenge students to write four additional parts, either human or animal.

•   Introduce the concepts of puns. Have students identify the puns in the story then create more.

•   Tell students to imagine this play had been set in a zoo's veterinarian's office. Ask: How might the play have been different?

Discriminates Between Fiction and Nonfiction

Have students discuss whether this is fiction or nonfiction and explain choices.

Vocabulary Development

Invite students to list new words they have learned from this play.

Literary Response

Have teams of students retell the story in correct sequence. Challenge students to find at least three places where pus are used.

Creates Graphic Sources to Gather and Organize Information

Take a survey of the different pets belonging to students in your class. Graph the results. Challenge students to create word problems for one another based on the graph they created.

Waiting Room

NOTE TO TEACHER

There are 20 parts in this play. The Beagle has the biggest part and should be assigned to a strong reader. Assign parts, then let students practice reading first silently, and then to a partner. Avoid asking students to read aloud without time to practice.

At the conclusion of the Reader's Theater, challenge students to add more characters, rewrite some of the parts, or to analyze the humor (why was it funny?).

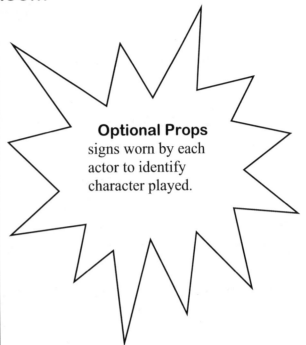

Optional Props
signs worn by each actor to identify character played.

Setting: a waiting room at a veterinarian's office

Cast of Characters

Beagle	Human 2
Mastiff	Human 3
Chihuahua	Duck
Ferret	Vet Receptionist
Iguana	Finch
Persian Cat – Mom	Rabbit
Persian Kitten 1	Alley Cat
Persian Kitten 2	Poodle
Persian Kitten 3	Vet Technician
Human 1	Cow

Waiting Room

Beagle: Hey big fella, what are you in for?

Mastiff: I've got a problem with one of my teeth. (paw at mouth) Hurts like everything.

Beagle: Gosh, you wouldn't think a little tooth could bring a big guy like you down.

Mastiff: Well, it does. What are you in for?

Beagle: Oh, I'm just in for my yearly check-up. When you stick your nose into as many places as I do, you can't be too careful.

Chihuahua: (shaking nervously) Could you two please keep the noise down.

Beagle: What's your problem?

Chihuahua: Nothing!

Beagle: Oh come on. You must be here for a reason.

Chihuahua: Well, if you must know, I am being treated for a nervous disorder.

Mastiff: A what?

Chihuahua: I get very nervous when I'm alone, and when I am around people, and other animals.

Beagle: So if you are nervous when you're alone, and around people, and animals, when are you not nervous?

Chihuahua: Bingo! That's just it. I'm nervous all the time. Now just leave me alone. Pretend I'm not here. (cover eyes with paws)

Ferret: (holding paw) I don't know what you all have to complain about. I'm the one with a real problem. I got my paw stuck in a mousetrap that was waaayyyy up under the refrigerator. It wasn't easy to get to, I can tell you that!

Mastiff: Then why did you try?

Ferret: Because it's my nature. I'm VERY curious.

Beagle: (looks disgusted) Oh brother!

Ferret: (looking up) Hey, what kind of animal are you?

Iguana: (speaking slowly and occasionally sticking tongue out) I am an iguana. I think that is pretty obvious.

Chihuahua: (shaking) Ask him to stop sticking out his tongue. He is making me nervous.

Beagle: What are you in for?

Iguana: That should also be obvious. I'm having a skin problem. I'm usually quite handsome.

Persian Cat - Mom: I'll have to take your word on that.

Iguana: Beauty is in the eyes of the beholder, madam.

Persian Kitten 1: (in a whiny voice) Where are we mom?

Persian Kitten 2: (in a tiny voice) Why are we here mom?

Persian Kitten 3: (in a small, upset voice and spitting) Get your tail out of my mouth!

Persian Cat - Mom: Behave you three! You are here for the first of your (spell out) S-H-O-T-S that will prevent you from getting some terrible diseases.

Persian Kitten 1: What does S-H-O-T-S mean?

Persian Kitten 2: Will it hurt mom?

Persian Kitten 3: Hey, that's MY ear you are chewing on!

Human 1: (frantic) Excuse me! Coming through! I have an emergency!

Ferret: What's he got wrapped up in that jacket? I've got to find out.

Beagle: (sniffing the air) Smells foul to me!

Human 1: This duck swallowed a fishhook. You can see the fishing line coming out of its mouth.

Duck: (choking sound and a quack) I just wanted a nice piece of bread, no strings attached, but NO! (choking again) I get a fishhook with this piece!

Human 1: I'm really sorry. I was using bread for bait. I didn't think about ducks liking bread, too.

Veterinary Receptionist: We'll take care of him. Will you just have a seat in the waiting room? I'll see what the veterinarian suggests we do.

Finch: (chirp, chirp) Humans really can be thoughtless sometimes. I know. This one time I was flying around the den and thought I saw some fresh fruit on the coffee table. You'll never believe what was inside the fruit!

Iguana: I'll bite. What was it made of?

Finch: Wax. Cold, solid, no taste, wax. I had stomach problems for a week. See what I mean about humans being thoughtless.

Rabbit: I don't think all humans are thoughtless. My human takes great care of me!

Ferret: Then why are you here?

Rabbit: To get my nails clipped.

Mastiff: You go to a doctor to have your nails clipped? (shaking head, unbelieving)

Rabbit: Well, my humans are very cautious. If you clip nails too closely it can cause a lot of pain and bleeding. My humans don't want that to happen, so I come in every couple of months to have the professionals do it.

Chihuahua: Stop talking of clipping nails. That makes me nervous, too!

Persian Kitten 1: Is it our turn next?

Persian Kitten 2: You sure it won't hurt?

Persian Kitten 3: Get off my face!

Persian Cat - Mom: Shhhhhhhh! It won't be much longer.

Iguana: Check out the new guy.

Alley Cat: (acts angry and tough) You talkin' to me?! You talkin' to me?! Hey, you talkin' to me?!

Iguana: Yes, obviously, you just came in. I am talking to you.

Alley Cat: (talking to Persian Cat) Hey mama, how ya doin'?

Ferret: So new guy, what are you here for?

Alley Cat: None of ya business. How's that for an answer?!

Human 2: I'm here to drop off my male cat to be neutered. When should I come back to pick him up?

Persian Kitten 1: What does neuter mean, mom?

Persian Kitten 2: Does that hurt?

Persian Kitten 3: Get me out of this basket!

Veterinarian Receptionist: He'll be ready first thing in the morning. Have a nice day!

Alley Cat: Yeah! (shaking head) Nice day for you maybe.

Human 1: Have you heard anything about the duck yet?

Veterinarian Technician: Yes, the vet says it was great that you brought the duck in. She said many people would feel too guilty or not care and just leave the duck. She wants to know if you would be willing to take it back to its home as soon as she is finished. It won't be much longer and there will be no charge.

Human 1: Sure, that's the least I can do.

Rabbit: See what I mean. There are lots of nice humans around.

Human 3: I'm here to pick up my sweet little poodle, Foxy Lady. I left her here while I went to Paris and I'm ready to take her home now.

Veterinarian Technician: I'll bring her right out.

Poodle: (very spoiled sounding) Don't ever leave me here again! There's nothing but animals here! I didn't like the food and the accommodations were practically nonexistent! No cushions! No television! No snacks! I had to WALK on the cement in the sun! (whining and whimpering)

Finch: Check out the pink bows on her ears!

Poodle: Do you see what I mean? This is the kind of harassment I've heard all week! If I don't get home soon, I think I will just faint from all the stress!

Duck: Okay, where is the big, brave fisherman? You owe me a ride back home buddy, and a MAJOR apology!

Chihuahua: It is getting too crowded in this waiting area. I'm really getting nervous now.

Rabbit: You think it's crowded now. Look what's coming through the door everybody!

Cow: Moooooooooove out of my way! I'm about to have a cow!

Everyone Scatters!

Pre-Reading Suggestions:

Assessing Prior Knowledge
Draw a simple outline of an automobile and divide it into three sections. Use the first section to assess what students already know about the history of the automobile industry. Use the other sections to record what students want to know, and what they learned.

Making Predictions
Tell students the play they will read is a brief history of the automobile industry. Ask students to discuss the following: If they had written this play where would they have started and how would they tell the story.

Identifies Facts and Details
Explain this play is written in seven acts. Each act covers a particular span of time. Challenge students to record facts or details that don't really fit the time period. Have students hold the notes for discussion at the end of the play.

Post-Reading Suggestions:

Acts 1-4

Making Predictions
Ask students to share the prediction they made before the play began. Where did this play begin and how is the author telling the story of the automobile industry?

Identifies Facts and Details
Have students begin filling in the middle section of the car outline, "What I Learned". Ask students if they heard anything in Act 1 that did not seem to fit with the time period? (cave people talking in a developed language, reference to wife, etc.)

- What about Act 2? (there were no travel games to buy then)
- What about Act 3? (the words *automobile* and *American Dream* weren't used then)
- What about Act 4? (people probably didn't "high-five" back then)

Expressing Ideas in Writing
In Act 4, Frank Duryea says that having his car break down during the first public test was the most embarrassing moment in his life. Have students write a paragraph describing their most embarrassing moment. Assure students they will not have to share unless they wish.

Post-Reading Suggestions cont.:

Retells a story including important events and details

Have students form four groups. Assign each group one of the four acts of the play. Have them reread then organize and plan how they will retell that part of the story to the rest of the class.

Acts 5-7

Identifies Facts and Details

Complete filling in the middle section of the car outlines, "What I Would Like to Know".

Independent Reading and Research

Fill in the final sections of the car, "What I Learned". Leave this section up in a corner of the room. Furnish reference books that may help discover the answers to these questions. This can be an ongoing project. Be sure to have students share their discoveries at some point.

Expressing Ideas in Writing

Have students work in groups of three or four to discuss what might be in Act 8. Have them write a brief outline or summary that they will share with the class. After all ideas have been shared and discussed have students go back to their group and write Act 8.

Sequential Order

Have students form three groups. Have each group illustrate six to eight major events that happened during the development of the automobile. Place the drawings in sequential order and display.

In the Beginning There Was the Wheel

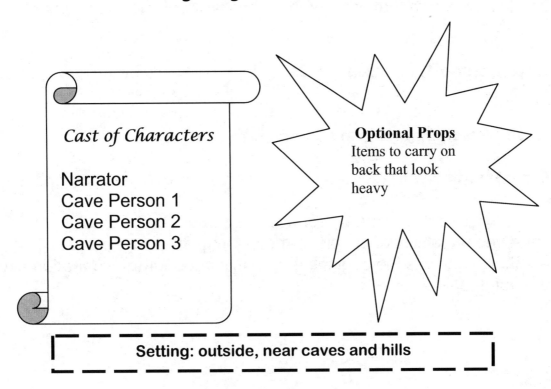

Cast of Characters

Narrator
Cave Person 1
Cave Person 2
Cave Person 3

Optional Props
Items to carry on
back that look
heavy

Setting: outside, near caves and hills

Act I

Narrator: (standing to the left of the stage.) In the beginning, man lived in caves with his family and a few close friends and relatives. There wasn't much need for an automobile because there really wasn't any place to go. There was, however, the need for the wheel. The time is 12,000 B.C.

Cave Person 1: (carrying what seems like a heavy burden) I can't believe that I, Grog, have to carry heavy burdens over hills to my wife, Grogina, and little Grogletts.

Cave Person 2: (carrying a heavy burden also) I hear that! Must be an easier way to get things from one place to other.

Cave Person 3: (carrying a heavy burden) How about cart with wheels?

Cave Person 1: (stops to look at Cave Person 3.) What's that?

Cave Person 3: (stops, scratches head, and looks very puzzled) I don't know where that came from. (shrugs shoulders) Just forget I said that!

Cave Person 1: (speaking to Cave Person 2) He's losing it! Must be the heat!

Cave Person 2: (grunts in agreement)

Cave People: (walk off stage, continuing to carry heavy burdens)

Narrator: Eventually the wheel was developed, and it greatly improved the ability of people to move things from one place to another. That was the beginning of man's need for transportation and the automobile.

Act II

NOTE TO TEACHER

Preparation

Make 3 large signs that read "100 Years". You may opt to have students create the signs before the play begins.

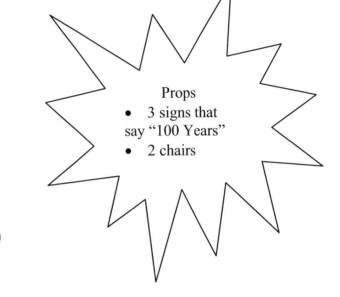

Props
- 3 signs that say "100 Years"
- 2 chairs

Cast of Characters
Narrator
Pioneer Man
Pioneer Woman
Two Pioneer Children
Three Sign Carriers

Setting: riding in a covered wagon on the plains

Narrator: Hundreds of years went by. (three students with signs that say "100 Years" walk across the stage) People started harnessing animals to the wheels because that made moving objects and people much easier. Hundreds of years went by. (same three students with signs walk across the stage) People discovered other people in different parts of the world, so they decided to visit. Some even moved their entire families. Carriages were invented (100 Years walks by), then stagecoaches (100 Years walks by), then the covered wagon. The need for the automobile was getting greater and greater. The time is now 1750. I told you hundreds of years went by!

(Two pioneers sit in chairs at the front of the "covered wagon," and two pioneer children sit on the floor behind them.)

Pioneer Man: (holding imaginary reins to the horses.) Things are sure going to be different when we get to Texas. No more busy streets like ours where sometimes as many as three carriages pass by our house within an hour.

Pioneer Woman: (sitting next to Pioneer Man.) Yes sirree! We'll have a piece of land that nobody else has ever seen. Nobody will drop by for days, weeks, or even months.

Pioneer Children: (tap pioneer parents on the shoulders and take turns saying lines.)
    Are we there yet?
    I'm hungry!
    I'm bored!
    I want to go back home.
    Didn't you buy any travel games for us to play?

Pioneer Man: (turning around and acting frustrated) Now settle down back there! We've got miles to go yet. Don't make me come back there! If you two don't sit still, I'm gonna turn this wagon around...

Narrator: Some say this was the start of the American family vacation.

Act III

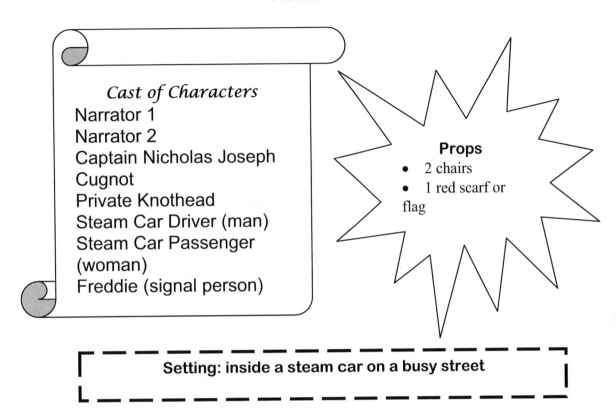

Cast of Characters
Narrator 1
Narrator 2
Captain Nicholas Joseph Cugnot
Private Knothead
Steam Car Driver (man)
Steam Car Passenger (woman)
Freddie (signal person)

Props
- 2 chairs
- 1 red scarf or flag

Setting: inside a steam car on a busy street

Narrator 1: The first road vehicle that could travel by itself was a steam car. Just imagine a great big teakettle with three wheels. It was invented in 1769 by French army captain Joseph Cugnot.

Narrator 2: It hauled cannons, traveled just 3 miles per hour, and had to stop every 10 or 15 minutes to build up steam.

Captain Cugnot: (*speaks with a French accent, is seated in a chair with Private Knothead pretending to walk beside him*) What do you think of my invention now, Private Knothead? (*car stops to build up steam, Private Knothead stops pretending to walk*)

Private Knothead: (*speaks with a French accent*) It is great, sir! At this rate we might actually get to the battle before everyone goes home. (*start pretending to walk*)

Captain Cugnot: (slightly annoyed at the private's comment) Say what you will, but I plan to get rich off this invention, and I want to be alive to spend it! People are going to become very dependent on the automobile. You mark my words!

Narrator 1: Steam-powered vehicles that could carry passengers were developed in England around 1801. Unfortunately steam carriages annoyed many people. These early cars were noisy, frightened horses, dirtied the air with smoke, and scattered hot coals. Sometimes the coals set fire to crops or wooden bridges.

Narrator 2: A law was passed in 1865 that limited the speed of steam vehicles to 4 miles per hour on country roads and 2 miles per hour in cities. The law also required a signalman to walk ahead of each steam carriage to warn of its approach. The signalman carried a red flag during the day and red lantern at night.

Steam Car Driver: *(sitting in a chair bouncing up and down slowly, holding the steering wheel with one hand and brake handle with the other; the signalman, is walking in front, waving a red flag and stomping out hot coals)* Dear, since we can only drive 2 miles an hour now, don't you think it would be just as easy to walk to church on Sundays? After all, we only live two blocks away, and we have to wake Freddie up to be our signalman on his one day off. Freddie, get that hot coal that just flew onto the dentist's porch! *(Freddie runs to stomp it out and then gets back to the front of the car)*

Steam Car Passenger: *(looking snobbish)* Absolutely not! I wouldn't dream of letting Gertrude see me walk when we have a perfectly beautiful Stanley Steamer parked in our barn. Don't be ridiculous! We depend on our car for more than just getting from one place to the other or carrying heavy loads. Cars send people a message. Our car says, "Look at how well we are doing!" That's an important part of the American Dream, you know. Stop being so practical!

Steam Car Driver: *(pointing frantically)* Freddie, there goes another one! Get it quick! I can't afford to rebuild the school again!

Freddie: *(yawning from lack of sleep, waving a red scarf or flag, stomping out flying hot coals)* Steam car coming through! Steam car coming through!

Narrator 1: Steam cars didn't last past the early 1900s.

Narrator 2: Besides the obvious drawbacks, many people were just plain scared to drive a vehicle that depended on an open fire and hot steam!

Act IV

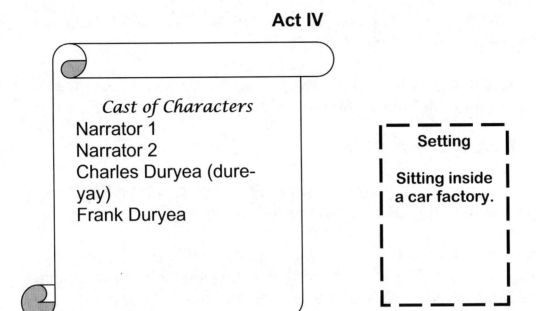

Cast of Characters
Narrator 1
Narrator 2
Charles Duryea (dure-yay)
Frank Duryea

Setting

Sitting inside a car factory.

Narrator 1: The electric car gained some popularity during the late 1890s and early 1900s. Electric cars were easy to operate, ran quietly, and did not give off smelly fumes or dangerous sparks.

Narrator 2: On the down side, however, few went faster than 20 miles per hour and their batteries had to be recharged about every 50 miles. It was a great improvement over the steam car, but quickly lost its popularity with the invention of the gasoline-powered car.

Narrator 1: Most experts agree that the Duryea brothers, Charles and Frank, built the first successful American gasoline-powered automobile.

Narrator 2: They also established the first American company for the manufacturing of gasoline-powered automobiles.

Charles Duryea: *(clapping brother on shoulder and shaking hands)* Well, brother, congratulations on a job well done. We'll be sittin' pretty now. We'll make a future.

Frank Duryea: *(shaking hands and looking happy)* Congratulations to you too, brother. I was a little worried there for a while when our car broke down during its first public test. It was one of my most embarrassing moments. But I guess you're right. We can kick back and just wait for the money to roll in.

Charles: *(looking concerned)* Then you aren't worried about those three guys we heard about the other day?

Frank: *(looking puzzled.)* Who are you talking about?

Charles: A man by the name of Henry Ford, another man named Henry Leland, and a third man named Ransom Eli Olds.

Frank: Are you kidding? We are famous. It wasn't Ford, Leland, or Olds who won the "Race of the Century." It was us in our two-cylinder Duryea Motor Wagon. We are celebrities. We started our own company and have built 13 cars this year.

Charles: That's right, and don't forget one of our cars is being used in the Barnum & Bailey circus. We are kings of the automobile industry! *(Charles high-fives his brother.)*

Act V

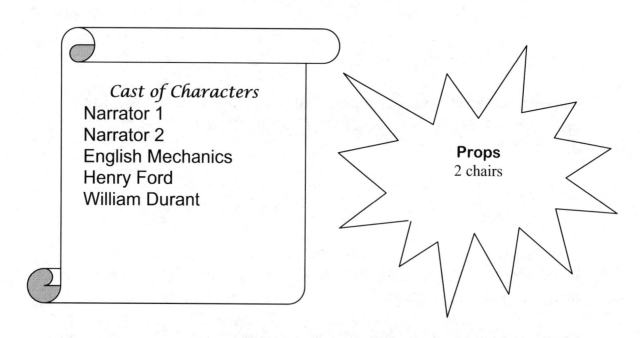

Cast of Characters
Narrator 1
Narrator 2
English Mechanics
Henry Ford
William Durant

Props
2 chairs

Narrator 1: The Duryea brothers did make a valuable contribution to the automobile industry, but that was all. Because of envy and greed, their partnership and friendship ended soon after they won the race.

Narrator 2: By 1900, more than 100 brands of cars, or horseless carriages as they were called then, were being built and sold in the United States. Because early cars had to be handmade, they were very expensive. Most people hated to see horseless carriages come their way. The cars scared horses, turned over vegetable carts, hit people, and were resented by poor and middle-class people who couldn't afford them. In spite of the problems, the car gained popularity.

Narrator 1: The Duryea brothers should have worried more about Olds, Leland, and Ford. Ransom Eli Olds, founder of the Olds Motor Works in Detroit, built 425 gasoline-powered automobiles in 1901. This was the beginning of mass production and the assembly line.

Narrator 2: Interchangeable parts for cars were developed by Henry M. Leland, president of the Cadillac Automobile Company. This means that you could put a part from one car into any other car of the same model. To prove his point, he sent jumbled parts of three Cadillac's in a large box to some mechanics in England.

English Mechanic: (speaking with an English accent) When I opened that box, I thought the bloke had gone daft, goofy in the head. No way could me friends, the best automobile technicians in all of Europe, put this mess together into three complete cars. But we did, by George! Right snappy looking vehicles too, if I do say so myself.

Narrator 1: Henry Ford improved the assembly line methods, invented the moving assembly line, and figured out ways to cut the cost of making a car.

Narrator 2: In 1908, Ford reached his goal. The Model T Ford took little more than an hour-and-a-half to build and sold for around $850.

Henry Ford: (seated in what could be a car) Yes, my cars were the most popular cars in America for nearly 20 years. It could have stayed that way too, if it hadn't been for a man named William C. Durant. Who would have ever guessed that a carriage maker would buy Cadillac, Oldsmobile, Buick, Pontiac, and Chevrolet, then form a company called General Motors? As if that weren't bad enough, he went and invented the electric starter. What was wrong with hand-cranking to start a car? Good exercise if you ask me! (looks disgusted and turns the key to start the car, grimacing as if turning the key is too simple a way to start a car)

William Durant: (seated in what could be a car, facing Henry Ford) It wasn't just the starter, Henry. Sure you made the least expensive car on the market and cost was certainly important to lots of people, but you forgot about style and comfort. You kept cranking out those plain Tin Lizzies, our Chevrolet, at a higher price, outsold Ford in 1927. The Model T was a good try, but since 1929 we've outsold Ford every year.

Act VI

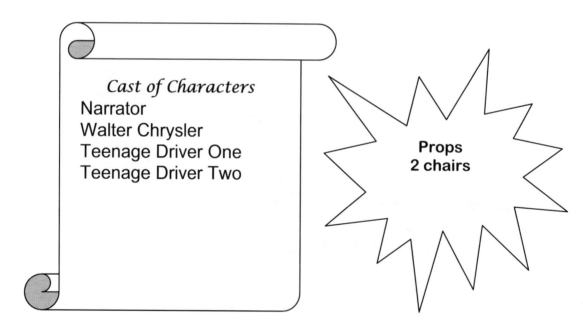

Cast of Characters
Narrator
Walter Chrysler
Teenage Driver One
Teenage Driver Two

Props
2 chairs

Narrator: By the 1920s, only the large manufacturers that could make and sell many cars quickly were able to stay in business. The number of U.S. automakers dropped. Gradually, three huge companies took over the manufacturing of most American cars: General Motors, Ford, and Chrysler. Meet Walter Chrysler.

Walter Chrysler: Ford and GM were so worried about each other that they didn't even notice when I bought Dodge, De Soto, and Plymouth. Of course, GM was still tough to beat. We never could top Chevrolet sales. GM brought in a new man, Alfred Sloan. According to him, Ford was putting people on wheels, but GM was enticing them to get fancier wheels. That's when cars got longer, lower, wider, and more powerful. People loved their automobiles!

Teenage Driver One: (leaning on chair as if leaning on the side of a car) I look cool hanging out near the corner drugstore with my dad's car. I've got a car with an automatic transmission.

Teenage Driver Two: (leaning on chair is if learning on the side of a car) I look more cool hanging out near the corner drugstore with my dad's car. I have an automatic transmission AND an AM/FM radio.

Driver One: Well, I've got automatic transmission, AM/FM radio, AND power brakes.

Driver Two: Oh yeah! Well, I've got automatic transmission, AM/FM radio, power brakes, AND power steering.

Driver One: So What! I've got automatic transmission, AM/FM radio, power brakes, power steering, AND tinted windows.

Driver Two: Big deal! I've got automatic transmission, AM/FM radio, power brakes, power steering, tinted window, AND air conditioning.

Driver One: Big whoop! I've got automatic transmission, AM/FM radio, power brakes, power steering, tinted windows, air conditioning, AND my dad's credit card that I can use any time I want to put gas in the car.

Driver Two: Okay, you win! (both drivers get in imaginary cars and drive away)

Act VII

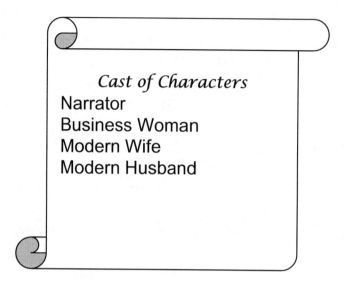

Cast of Characters
Narrator
Business Woman
Modern Wife
Modern Husband

Narrator: For many years, the United States produced more cars than all other countries combined. Now, it makes about one third of the world's automobiles. The big three – GM, Ford, and Chrysler – now have to compete with foreign car manufacturers.

Business Woman: Hold on there. That's not such a bad thing. Competition brings out the best. Thanks to the foreign car industry, we learned to save one of our limited natural resources, oil. After Americans started buying foreign cars that got good gas mileage, the American automobile industry stopped trying to make the longest, shiniest, fastest cars and started trying to make smaller, lighter cars that used less fuel. With foreign cars being sold and repaired by Americans in our country, and the fact that families continue to have a second and even a third and a fourth car, there seems to be enough business for everyone.

Modern Wife: (looking at checkbook and speaking to husband) You know, with my new promotion, we can afford to pay off William Junior's car and buy a fourth car so Tracey can have one, too. What do you think?

Modern Husband: (looking a bit surprised) I think paying off Junior's car is a great idea, but I'm not so sure Tracey needs a car.

Modern Wife: (looking annoyed) Are you saying a boy should have a car, but a girl should not?

Husband: (looking annoyed) No, dear, I'm not saying that. It's just that because Tracey is only 9, it seems like we could wait a while longer. Don't you think?

Narrator: Cars already go faster than the law allows, and there are automobiles to suit just about anyone's personality and budget. That leaves only two other areas to conquer in the story of the automobile – safety and alternative fuels for a cleaner environment. It will be exciting to see what the next 100 years brings. We've come a long way since the wheel was invented!

Penny for Your Thoughts. . .

What do you think you will be driving when you are a teenager? When you're 40? When you're 60? What will your grandchildren drive?

Pre-Reading Suggestions:

Assessing Prior Knowledge

Create a K-W-L chart. Ask students to fill in the first two columns of the chart. What do they already know about the rainforest? What would they like to know about the rainforest?

Challenge students to brainstorm a list of vocabulary words that would be associated with the study of a rainforest.

Post-Reading Suggestions

Drawing Conclusions

Have students fill in the remaining column on the K-W-L chart. Ask: What did you learn about the rainforest?

Expressing Ideas in Writing

Challenge students to work in small groups to rewrite the ending to the play. Allow time for sharing with the class.

Challenge students to create four additional parts for this play.

Have students write a paragraph identifying which animal they would be if they lived in the rainforest and why.

Vocabulary development

Have students brainstorm new words they have learned from this play.

Geography Research

Have students research the amount of rain that falls during a one-year period in a rainforest.

Have students draw pictures showing the amount of sunlight that shines in each layer of the rainforest?

Challenge students to show where the world's rainforests are located.

Have students draw then identify the four layers of a rainforest and list or draw some of the plants and animals that can be found in each layer.

Rainforest
Detour

Cast of Characters

Cat	Anteater
Spider Monkey 1	Boa Constrictor
Spider Monkey 2	Iguana 1
Bat	Iguana 2
Howler Monkey 1	Puma
Howler Monkey 2	Capybara
Parrot 1	Sloth
Parrot 2	Katydid 1
Ant bird	Katydid 2

Optional Props
Signs worn by each actor to identify character played.

Setting: An airplane has just dropped off a pet carrier with a drowsy cat inside. The carrier was left on an airstrip in the middle of a rainforest. Many animals are curious about the creature inside.

Rainforest
Detour

Parrot 1: ROK! Would you look at that? What is that?

Parrot 2: Hey, there's something inside, ROK!

Parrot 1: You should go see what it is.

Parrot 2: No way. Let's send someone else. Hey, spider monkey, go see what's in that box over there.

Spider Monkey 1: Sure. We were wondering what's in there, too. (leaps to the pet carrier)

Cat: (a long, mean meow and a couple of hisses)

Spider Monkey 2: Better get away from it quick! Sounds like some sort of tiger or jaguar.

Cat: (yawns and stretches) I most certainly am not a tiger or jaguar, though I am a member of the feline family. May I inquire who you are and what you are doing staring at me?

Spider Monkey 1: We weren't staring, we were just curious. We've never seen anything like you in the rainforest.

Cat: The what forest? You mean this isn't San Francisco?

Spider Monkey 2: Nope! You're in trouble, kitty. San Francisco is about 1,500 miles that way (pointing) or that way (pointing in the opposite direction).

Cat: Oh my gosh! That's not good. I ate my last Classy Cat tender morsels cheese snack and am completely out of my cat nip. What shall I eat? Where shall I live? Who shall look after me? I've never been on my own before.

Spider Monkey 1: Hey, we can help. We can tell you about where we live and what we eat, and then you can decide where you want to live but you are going to have to take care of yourself! That's what being "wild" is all about.

Cat: While I am not "wild" about that idea, I suppose I need to do something. Where do you live?

Spider Monkey 2: We live in the trees at the canopy and sometimes the emergent layers of the rainforest, and we eat the fruits we find there. How does that sound?

Cat: Well, I think I could get used to living in the trees, as long as I don't have to go too high. I don't know about fruit. I think I'm more of a carnivore than an herbivore. Anybody like that around here?

Anteater: Look no further! I live on the forest floor, and I eat juicy, tasty ants.

Ant bird: If I didn't know better, I would swear you were a pig instead of an anteater. You hog all of the tasty ants on the forest floor so I have to eat the ones that climb the trees in the understory layer.

Anteater: Too bad, sweetheart. You snooze, you lose!

Cat: It sounds like there's too much competition for your food, so I think I'll keep looking. Thanks anyway.

Boa: Sssssssssay, how would you like to sssseeee where I live and sssssleeep? It'sssssssss the besssst place around!

Sloth: (speaking very slowly) Yeah, right! Go with him, and it will be the last time we see you. Come live with me. I'll teacher you to hang upside down to do EVERYTHING.

Cat: Living with the snake is definitely out, and I don't think I could ever learn to hang upside down to sleep. But thank you both for your offers.

Bat: Hey, up here. I'm a bat and, like you, I'm nocturnal. Could you guys hold it down? I'm trying to sleep. Tonight, I'll teach you to search for nectar. Nectar is delicious!

Cat: But you hang upside down to sleep, too. Besides, I can't fly.

Howler Monkey 1: (shouting) Hey! I think she should come live with us! She would fit right in. Howl!

Howler Monkey 2: (shouting) I think we could even teach her to howl and swing in the trees. Howl!

Cat: I hate to interrupt (hands over ears), but I don't think I could ever get used to the volume at which you speak. Don't you ever talk quietly?

Howler Monkeys: NO!!!! Howl!

(The sound of katydids)

Cat: Excuse me, but who just made that noise?

Katydid 1: Katydid.

Cat: Oh. What are you?

Katydid 2: Katydid.

Cat: No, I want to know what kind of animal you are.

Iguana 1: They just told you.

Cat: Told me what?

Katydids: (shouting) KATYDID!

Cat: Katy did what?

Iguana 2: They are katydids. They just say "katydid" all day, every day. You wouldn't be happy trying to talk to them or doing anything else with them. Why don't you come live with me? I live on and near the forest floor and eat insects.

Cat: Insects don't agree with my delicate stomach, but thanks anyway. (*saying to herself*) Is everyone creepy here or what?

Capybara: I'm the largest rodent in the world, and I eat grass. How does that sound?

Cat: WOW!!!! I have my answer! You are, beyond a doubt, the largest rodent I have ever seen.

Capybara: I'm not a rodent. I'm a capybara.

Cat: (looking disappointed and discouraged) Well, when I eat grass, I usually do it to cough up a fur ball. I think I'm running out of options.

Puma: I suppose I could let you join my family, though we don't eat cat food. We track our food, kill it, then eat the parts we want, and leave the rest. We live wherever we want.

Cat: I don't think that will work for me either. Killing for my food would be gross! I can't even watch the nature channel. Eating dead things-Blaaaa!

All Animals: What's that? I hear something! Sounds like a plane.

Cat: Oh, thank goodness…they've come back for me! I could never live here! Hurry! Please! (gets back in cage…plane lands and picks up the cat)

Monkey 1: Don't forget to write!

Monkey 2: (rolling eyes at Monkey 1) Like you could read it.

Pre-Reading Suggestions

Assessing Prior Knowledge

Say: This play is entitled "Famous Folks". What makes someone famous? What is the difference between famous and infamous?

Challenge students to list as many famous people as they can in 10 minutes (have students work with a partner or small group and adjust the time limit as appropriate for age level). Next, have students place each person listed in categories such as, athletes, scientists, entertainers, etc.

Post-Reading Suggestions

Expressing Ideas in Writing

Have students work in small groups to rewrite the ending to the play. Encourage them to share their creations with the group.

Invite students to use the Famous Folks Independent Research sheet as a guide to help them add another character to this play.

Ask: If you could invite four famous folks (living or dead) to have lunch with you, who would you invite and why? Have students write a skit or play with the dialogue from such a meeting that could happen around the table.

Vocabulary development

Have students list new words they learned from this play.

Timelines

Challenge students to create a time line that includes all the people in the "Famous Folks" play.

Famous Folks
Independent Research

Directions:
Select a famous person to research. Read at least one biography and research one additional source. Use the following research form:

Famous Person: _____

Why is this person famous? _____

_____

_____

What is unique about this person?_____

_____

_____

_____

When did this person live? _____

Script to be inserted in the Reader's Theater:

_____

_____

Where should the script be inserted and how will it connect to the flow of the play?

_____

Famous Folks

Cast of Characters

Student 1	Ulysses Grant
Student 2	General Lee
George Washington	Abraham Lincoln
Martha Washington	
Benjamin Franklin	
Thomas Edison	
George Washington Carver	
Johnny Appleseed	
Maria Tallchief	
Kerri Strug	
Lance Armstrong	
Troy Aikman	
Michael Jordan	
Jane and Ann Taylor	
Elvis Presley	
Florence Nightingale	
Robert Goddard	
Neil Armstrong	

Optional Props
Signs worn by
each actor to
identify them.

Setting: after school waiting to be picked up by parents

Famous Folks

Student 1: (walk out grumbling to yourself holding three biography books)

Student 2: What are you grumbling about?

Student 1: Well, I got a "B" in spelling today, my peanut butter sandwich was stale, and if that wasn't bad enough Mrs. _____ (teacher's name) said we have to read three biographies!

Student 2: What's wrong with biographies: I LOVE them!!!

Student 1: You've got to be kidding!!

(George and Martha Washington Enter behind Student 2's back)

You like reading about old, boring people?

George: Excuse me young man (tapping student on the shoulder) who are you calling boring?
Martha: (looking annoyed) AND OLD?

Student 1: (looking at other student a little cautious) Where did they come from?

Student 2: Your imagination of course. This happens to me all the time.

George: Don't try to change the subject, young man. What did you mean boring? (pause – then facing audience in an arrogant manner) Didn't you know I was the first President of the United States, the Commander-in-Chief of the American Army, responsible for the first census ever taken, creator of the National Bank, and am called "The Father of this Country"?

Martha: Don't forget the cherry tree incident.

George: (embarrassed) Martha you know that's not really true. Besides they built a monument to me and named the capital after me and don't forget the George Washington Birthday Sales in February!

Martha: Yes, but your picture is only on the one dollar bill (looking at audience) and we all know how far that goes nowadays!

George: Martha!

Student 2: Excuse me, do you know any other famous folks you could introduce us to?

Martha: Sure, we know lots of them. Who would you like to meet?

Both Students: (look at each other and shake their heads because can't decide who to meet first)

Martha: How about Benjamin Franklin? (looking at George) He was an inventor, philosopher, author, editor, diplomat, and a HUMORIST.

George: (looking jealous-rolls eyes)

Martha: (calling off stage) Oh, Ben…

Ben: (walks out eating a large loaf of unsliced bread with another loaf under arm) Hi Lady Washington, George. Looks like a storm brewing, great day for flying a kite!

Martha: (excitedly) Ben, tell the children here how you invented the lightning rod.

Ben: (shyly) Oh Martha, you know what I always say: "God helps them that help themselves".

(The Washington's take a seat)

Student 2: Mr. Franklin, you sure did a lot of things in your life time.

Ben: Well, as I always say, "Never leave that till tomorrow which you can do today". Would you like to meet another inventor?

Student 1: Sure!

Ben: Tom, Thomas Edison, come on out here and meet
_____ (Student 1 name) and _____ (Student 2 name).

Tom: Hi Ben (shake hands) Hello _____ (Student 1 name) and _____ (Student 2 name)

Ben: Well, I have to go now, as I always say, "Early to bed and early to rise, makes a man healthy, wealthy and wise". (leave yawning and eating bread)

Tom: Which invention would you like me to show you?

Student 1: How about the electric light bulb?

Tom: Oh, that's all anybody cares about. How about my first invention, the electric vote recorder?

Student 2: No, the light bulb.

Tom: Nobody liked my vote counter. (sad...then happy) How about my telegraph, mimeograph, dictating machine, electric pen, motion picture camera and projector, ticker-tape machine...?

Student 2: (shaking head) No, the light bulb.

Tom: (taking bulb out of coat pocket) I know, the light bulb.

(phone rings)

Tom: (reaches into pocket and pulls out cell phone) Excuse me, hello...Sure I'll be right there Alexander. See you kids – gotta run – Mr. Bell wants to talk to me about some new invention of his. I think I saw George Washington Carver coming down the road though. He was also an inventor. (walk off)

Carver: (walk in) Hello children, sorry to hear about your peanut butter sandwich being stale _____ (name of Student 1) –

here (reaches into pocket and pulls out sandwich) I always carry an extra with me.

Student 1: (looking a little skeptical) Gee thanks!

Carver: Sure, you know …I found almost 300 uses for the common peanut. Funny…I never got as much attention as former President Jimmy Carter and all he did was grow them.

Student 1: Besides being famous for your work in the laboratory weren't you also a well known painter and poet?

Carver: Why, yes I was dear, do you like to paint and write poetry.

Student 2: Yes, very much.

Carver: Well, I have to go now. I'm working on the soybean.

Student 1 and 2: Bye – good luck with the soybean.

Martha: Talking about all that food has made me hungry. I could use a bit of nourishment.

Appleseed: (skips in) At your service ma'am! Johnny, John Chapman's the name – Apples are my game. (hands everyone an apple) You can make pies, tarts, jam, jelly, pudding, applesauce, or dumplings, (looking at audience) Of course I like 'em raw. (takes big bite and skips off)

Student 1: (looking at apple) I'm really beginning to like famous people now.

Maria: (comes spinning out) I'm Maria Tallchief. The first American ballerina to gain international fame, I showed the world that American Ballet could equal European dancing in quality! (Goes dancing off)

Kerri: (comes out, does a somersault or cartwheel) And I'm Kerri Strug. I am a two-time Olympian and gold medallist but I'm best known for bringing victory to the 1996 Olympic gymnastic team by sticking my vault landing with an injured ankle.

Lance: (bikes out wearing bright yellow shirt and wrist band) So how is your ankle now Kerri? I'm Lance Armstrong, winner of seven Tour de France competitions.

Student 2: Oh yes, (getting excited) I recognize you. You overcame a huge medical issue that almost took your life.

Lance: Yes, I was diagnosed with cancer but I got the help I needed and am cancer free now. I started the Lance Armstrong Foundation where we say unity is strength, knowledge is power and attitude is everything. LIVE STRONG!!!! (rides off as students wave goodbye)

Student 2: Who would you like to…

Student 1: Hey, it's Troy Aikman, famous quarterback for the Dallas Cowboys and one of the newest members of the Football Hall of Fame.

Troy: Oh, (shyly) I wouldn't say famous exactly but you might have seen me on television as a sport announcer recently.

Student 2: Oh yes, of course, and you are also known for all your philanthropic work with children.

Student 1: (speaking to Student 2) What is philanthropic work?

Student 2: Charity work and generosity.

Student 1: Way cool man!

Troy: If you want to meet a real legend in sports you need to meet this next guest in your imagination.

(Michael Jordan comes out.)

Hi Michael! (high fives Michael and Troy walks off stage)

Michael: Hey Troy. (Pointing to shoes) – nice Air Jordans! (Basketball out of control – hits Martha)

Martha: (Screams and runs from ball) Get that thing away from me! George who is that person? (point to Michael)

Michael: I hold the NBA record for most consecutive games scoring in double-digits, five-time NBA most valuable player, ranked 1st in NBA history in scoring averages, selected as one of the greatest players in NBA history; a member of six Chicago Bulls NBA Championships, shall I go on?

George: Very impressive. I just have one question though.

Michael: Shoot.

George: What is an NBA?

Michael: (walks off shaking his head in disbelief)

Jane and Ann: Hello _____(name of Student 1, waving and walking to center stage)

Student 1: Well, Hello Ann, Hello Jane. (turn to Student 1) That's Jane and Ann Taylor.

Student 2: I never heard of them.

Student 1: They are famous for writing children's poetry.

Student 2: Still haven't ever heard of them. What poems did they write?

Student 1: Let me give you a hint. They wrote a poem about a star and you have probably heard it a thousand times.

Student 2: (stands at attention and salutes) Oh, of course, the Star Spangled Banner!

Student 1: (laughing) No silly, that was Sir Frances Key, the Taylor sisters wrote *Twinkle, Twinkle, Little Star*.

Jane and Ann: (reciting) Twinkle, twinkle, little star. (hold star over head)
How I wonder what you are!
Up above the world so high,
Like a diamond in the sky.

When the blazing sun is gone,
When he nothing shines upon,
Then you show your little light
Twinkle, twinkle, all the night.

Bye now (waving as they leave)

Martha: Since we are speaking of literature, why don't we meet some famous men from music. There is Chopin, Mozart, Beethoven, the list is endless.

Student 2: Wow! There are so many. It would take all day to meet them all. Why don't we meet one of the most famous musician of all?

George: (to Martha) Care to dance my dear.

Martha: Thank you, I'd love to. (begin to waltz)

Student 2: (Elvis enters and Student 2 shouts) ELVIS PRESLEY!!!

Elvis: (comes out with the Elvis look on his face and wiggles one leg)

Martha: (fainting as George helps her to her chair)

Elvis: I often have that affect on women! (sings one verse of song, throws scarf to audience and waves to fans as he leaves)

Florence: (rushes out to Martha with lamp in her hand) Lady Washington. Are you alright?

George: I think she'll be fine. She just had a terrible shock.

Florence: I am Florence Nightingale, founder of modern methods of nursing. Yes, I could see she was suffering terribly.

George: Oh?

Florence: Yes, you may have heard of me referred to as "the lady with the lamp". I got this name by carrying a lamp on my hospital rounds.

Students 2: Miss Nightingale, weren't you also a women's rights activist?

Florence: If you mean, did I work for equal rights for women, you can bet your bloomers I did.

Martha: (regaining consciousness then faints again when she hears bloomers) Oh!

Florence: Well, I must go now and tend to more patients.

Student 2: That was sure exciting. (Goddard starts walking out looking at the rocket model in his hands) Oh, here comes someone else very exciting.

Student 1: Who is he?

Student 2: I'm surprised you don't know him. He is called the "Father of the Modern Rocket".

Goddard: Yes, I guess you could say I got the space program "OFF THE GROUND" (pause waiting for laughter) …Well, I always was a better scientist than a comedian. Let me introduce you to a man who has been very involved in the modern day space program, Astronaut Neil Armstrong.

Armstrong: (comes out) Nice to see you again Mr. Goddard. (shake hands) I've always admired your brilliant work.

Goddard: Thank you and I admired your courage being the first man to set foot on the moon.

Armstrong: Yes, but without your work that would have been impossible.

Goddard: Yes, but …

Student 2: Gentlemen please, we appreciate both of you.

Student 1: (shakes their hands) Yes, keep up the good work. (they leave) I know another pair in history that would be exciting to meet.

Student 2: Great, who are they?

Grant: General Ulysses S. Grant at your service. (salutes) Commander in Chief of the Northern armies in the War Between the States and 18th President of the United States.

Student 1: Nice to make your acquaintance sir, but I expected General Robert E. Lee to come out with you.

Grant: Oh, I asked him to come but he wouldn't. Stubborn pride!

Student 2: (looking off stage) General Lee…

Lee: (answering off stage where he can not be seen) He's not here!

Student 2: Please come out General Lee.

Lee: NO!

Student 2: But why sir?

Lee: The South lost the war between the States and I had to surrender to Grant.

Student 1: That's okay General Lee, we know you were a great leader and did the best you could under the circumstances. Besides it really worked out for the best.

Lee: (peeking around and comes out slowly) Really?

Grant: Sure Bob, now the states are all united.

Lee: Gee…I guess you're right. If I hadn't surrendered we may never have had baseball, hot dogs, apple pie and Toyotas…

Grant: (patting him on the back) That's right! Let's go have some chicken fried steak, collared greens, and biscuits dripping in gravy. The South always did have the best darn cooks!

Student 1: Well, I'm sure glad that had a happy ending.

George: Excuse me, but it seems to me you never did meet anyone else who comes up to my...shall we say...STANDARDS.

Student 1: That may be true General Washington but there is one more person I'd like _____(name of Student 2) to meet.

George: Oh, and who might that be?

Abe: Hello George, sorry I missed your birthday. Happy birthday.

George: Why Abe, good to see you! Happy Birthday to you, too.

Abe: I understand you're trying to decide who is the most famous historical figure?

George: Well, Abe, I've got to admit you sure did a lot for this country. And you do have a mighty nice monument in Washington, D.C., and don't forget the penny. (covers face and snickers)

Abe: Yes, I'm mighty proud of my face being on the penny. I always watched every penny I made and tried to tighten the pocket book while I served as president. As far as one most famous person though, I'm not sure there is one. We make each other great. Don't you agree George?

(Martha nudges George to make him agree)

George: Yes, Abe I'm sure you are right.

ACTION FREEZES

Student 2: Well _____(name of Student 1) how do you feel about biographies now?

Student 1: Are you kidding, I LOVE them! Let's go back to the library.

EVERYONE RETURNS TO THUNDEROUS APPLAUSE!

Optional: Have the entire cast sing "The Star-Spangled Banner" or other appropriate song.

Penny For Your Thoughts. . .
Who is your favorite character in this play? Which other
historical people would you have included and why?

Pre-Reading Activities:

Prediction
Have students think about what they already know of the past and brainstorm things that have evolved over the centuries, decades, and years.

Point of View
Ask students if progress is positive or negative. Have them examine both sides and explain situations in which progress could be seen as both positive and negative.

Assessing Prior Knowledge
Have students work in pairs or small groups to create an impromptu list, in sequential order, of inventions related to communication up to the present day.

Post-Reading Activities:

Vocabulary Development
Lead a discussion on the difference between the words "progress" and "change". Challenge students to write paragraphs explaining the difference.

Timelines
Challenge students to create a time line that summarizes the development of communication in America. Have students determine when the time line should begin.

Independent Research
Have students research then compare and contrast the communication systems we have available in our country with the types of communication systems found in other countries.

Prediction
Encourage students to make generalizations about how they believe communication will change over the next century.

Progress. . .Bah Humbug!

Note to Teacher

This short skit explains the changes in communication over time in a humorous way.

Have students add more parts to this Reader's Theater by researching more changes in communication.

Have students write a script about changes over time for some other topic such as: housing, medicine, transportation, clothing, sports equipment, modern conveniences like washing machines, manners, hobbies, architecture, entertainment, language, etc.

Cast of Characters

Senior Citizens 1 – 16

More characters can easily be added so every person has a speaking part.

Setting: senior citizens sitting around having a conversation in a retirement facility

Senior Citizen 1: My grandson sent me a new computer in the mail.

Senior Citizen 2: What for?

Senior Citizen 1: So I can blog.

Senior Citizen 3: What's blogging?

Senior Citizen 4: That's the way kids talk to each other these days.

Senior Citizen 1: No, that's e-mail. Blogging is newer. Blog is short for web log and is basically an online journal that you share with the world.

Senior Citizen 5: Sounds like the telegraph system to me. We had that when I was a young boy. Never used it much after we got the telephone.

Senior Citizen 2: Doesn't your grandson have a telephone?

Senior Citizen 1: Of course he does. He has a cell phone.

Senior Citizen 6: I have one of those. My kids sent me a fancy little cell phone so I could talk to them any time I want.

Senior Citizen 7: Yeah, my granddaughter sent me one of those things but it's so small I can't read the numbers. What was wrong with dialing the number? I don't like those push buttons!

Senior Citizen 8: I know what you mean. My kids sent me one, too. It is so small I can't find it most of the time and when I do find it the battery has run down.

Senior Citizen 9: What was wrong with the phone on the wall that you cranked and talked to a real person? The operator would even tell you who was new in town and who was sick.

Senior Citizen 10: What's so danged important that you have to talk to people all the time?

Senior Citizen 11: When I was a girl we didn't even have a crank phone. We wrote letters. We actually used pens and paper and it was fun to wait for a reply.

Senior Citizen 12: I haven't gotten a letter in years. I think people forgot how to write.

Senior Citizen 13: We lived so far from town we could only get our mail once a week if we were lucky.

Senior Citizen 14: Yeah, I remember getting news about family that was outdated before we got it.

Senior Citizen 15: Those were the days. Peace and quiet. Who needs this so-called progress?

Senior Citizen 1: Well, suit yourselves. I'm off to play my X-Box.

Senior Citizen 16: What's an X-Box.

Senior Citizen 1: Let's not go there! (sounding very frustrated)

Penny For Your Thoughts. . .

Communication has come a long way since the Pony Express. Imagine you are living in the year 2306. How do you think we will be communicating in that year?

Pre-Reading Activities:

Vocabulary Development
Tell students they will perform a reader's theater involving different breeds of dogs. Ask them to define breed and species.

Assessing Prior Knowledge
Tell students there are approximately 150 different breeds of dogs. Have students work with a partner or small group to brainstorm as many dog breeds as possible.

Point of View
Ask students if they have ever gone "shopping" for a new pet. Have them imagine what the animals are thinking when they see humans examining and watching them.

Post-Reading Activities:

Research
Every dog breed is assigned to one of seven groups or miscellaneous classes based on the uses for which the breeds were originally developed. Have students discover what those categories are.

Expressing Ideas in Writing
After determining why certain breeds were developed, have students consider the reason the need for a particular breed may now be obsolete. Have them write paragraphs explaining which breeds no longer serve their original purposes.

Ask: If you were going to create a new breed of dog, what purpose would this breed serve and what would you call it? Write a paragraph explaining your rationale then illustrate.

Mathematics
Have students go online and identify the cost for a puppy that is purebred. Then have students research and add the cost of veterinary needs, food, collar, bowl, leash, identification badge, and AKC (American Kennel Club) Registration. Compare and contrast the cost of a registered dog with that of an animal shelter adoption.

Pet Shop

Note to Teacher

This short skit explores a pet shop experience from a completely different point of view.

After reading the skit have students use the Pet Shop Independent Research sheet to explore the pros and cons of different pets living with different kinds of people in different environments.

Have students add more dog breeds to this Reader's Theater or completely rewrite the script using a variety of pets that may or may not include dogs.

Cast of Characters

Store Owner	Doberman
Assistant	St. Bernard
Customer	Golden Retriever
Beagle	Irish Setter
Pointer	Spaniel
Labrador	Chow
Collie 1	
Collie 2	

Optional Props
- Signs to identify breed of dog.
- Chairs to stand behind representing cages.

Setting: Pet Shop

Pet Shop

Directions:
Select an animal that could be a potential pet. Use the following research form:

Pet:

_____

Why would this animal be a good pet?_____

_____

What environment would be best for this type of pet?:_____

_____

_____

_____

Where is this animal originally from? _____

_____

In what way has this animal changed over time, if at all?_____

_____

Where and how script is to be inserted in the Reader's Theater:

_____

_____

_____

Pet Shop

Customer: Excuse me. I am looking for a dog. Can you help me?

Store Owner: Sure, I'll try to help you, but this isn't your usual pet shop. You see, in this pet shop the dog will pick YOU out. My assistant will show you around. (point to assistant)

Assistant: Hi, (shakes hands) I'm Tom. I'll show you around. Come with me.

Customer: (looking excited.) I can't wait to see what dog picks me!

Assistant: Don't let them hear you say "dog". They prefer the proper name Canidae from the Latin canis meaning "dog". Here is the first group.

Beagle: Hi! I'm Bob the beagle. (sniffs)

Pointer: I'm Bob's friend Pete. I'm a pointer. (points all over the room)

Beagle: We love to track things.

Pointer: We smelled you coming. (sniff louder)

Beagle: We were able to do this because we have long noses. That's how we are able to pick up scents so well.

Pointer: We can actually smell things better than we can see.

Beagle: Do you like to hunt?

Customer: No.

Pointer: Well, then we're not the dogs for you.

Assistant: Let's move on.

Labrador Retriever: Hi! My name is Elvis. I'm a Labrador Retriever and I love to swim! I'm the best swimmer you will find. I do it by just moving my front legs. You probably call it the "dog" paddle.

Customer: I don't like to swim.

Labrador Retriever: I would definitely not be happy with you. (walks away looking disappointed)

Assistant: Come on.

Collie 1: Hi! I'm Cary Collie.

Collie 2: I'm Candy Collie. You might have heard of my well-known cousin, Lassie.

Collie 1: My family dates back to 1,000 B.C.

Collie 2: We helped farmers herd sheep, goats, and cattle.

Collie 1: Even though we are mostly brown, farmers and shepherds preferred us white, so they would not confuse us with wolves and kill us by mistake. Do you have anything we can herd?

Customer: Just my brother and sister.

Collie 2: (shaking head in disappointment) Nope, that won't do.

Assistant: (frustrated) Let's move on.

Doberman Pinscher: (growls) I'm Spike. I'm a Doberman Pinscher. I like to guard things. I'm from Germany.

St. Bernard: I'm Beth. I'm a St. Bernard. I love to rescue people who get lost in the snow.

German Shepherd: I'm Sam Shepherd. I'm also from Germany and I help blind people get around safely. Some of my other family members help the police.

Doberman Pinscher: Growl! Growl!

St. Bernard: Spike! Stop that!

Doberman Pinscher: Sorry, old habit. Do you need us to help you with anything?

St. Bernard: Yes, please let us help.

German Shepherd: (looks anxious) I live to help!

Customer: No, I don't need any help. Sorry.

Golden Retriever: (has something in his mouth) Psssst! Hey kid, come here. I'm a golden retriever. I love to fetch things.

Irish Setter: Me too, laddie. Do ya happen to have a stick with ya?

Customer: (looks in pockets) No. (looks disappointed)

Golden Retriever: That's too bad. People call us sporting dogs. We retrieve and point out birds for hunters.

Irish Setter: Do you have a kennel, laddie?

Customer: No, I want my dog to live inside.

Golden Retriever: That won't do! We like it outside.

Customer: (looks very disappointed) This is not going very well!

Assistant: I have to admit you are a challenge, but we still have a few left.

Chow: I'm perfect for you. I'm a chow. I've been around for 3,000 years. You can run your fingers through my long thick hair and I can lick you with my blue-black tongue. I just love cold arctic breezes. You do live in a cold, arctic climate, don't you?

Customer: Well, not exactly.

Chow: Well, then I don't exactly want to own you.

Customer: This is really embarrassing.

Assistant: OK, there is one breed left, the toy. They are all 12 inches or shorter.

Spaniel: Hi! I'm a toy spaniel, a royal favorite. My ancestors owned King Charles. I'm from England originally and get along great with people. Do you have any royal blood?

Customer: No. Is that a problem?

Spaniel: (rolls eyes.) What do you think! (walks off with nose in air)

Store Owner: So how is it going? Any of the dogs like you?

Customer: No.

Store Owner: (looking sympathetic) Have you ever thought about a cat?

Pre-Reading Suggestions:

Assessing Prior Knowledge

Create a K-W-L chart. Ask students to fill in the first two columns of the chart. What do they already know about the zones of the ocean? What would they like to know about the zones of the ocean?

Challenge students to write about the kind of sea creature they would most like to be and where they think they would live in the ocean.

Post-Reading Suggestions:

Drawing Conclusions

Have students help you fill in the remaining column on the K-W-L chart. Ask: What did you learn about the ocean zones?

Expressing Ideas in Writing

Have students work in small groups to rewrite the ending to the play. Allow time for groups to share.

Have students revisit their writing from the pre-reading activity. Ask them to revise their writing telling about the ocean zone in which they would live.

Vocabulary development

Ask students to list new words they have learned from this play.

Research

Challenge students to draw then identify the five zones of the ocean and list or draw some of the plants and animals can be found in each zone.

Have students choose three of the following activities to complete:

- List the 5 oceans on Earth in order from smallest to largest.
- List the 5 oceans on Earth from shallowest to deepest.
- Differentiate between oceans and seas. Name at least 10 seas.
- Find out how much of the Earth's surface is covered by ocean.
- Describe and explain the many functions oceans on Earth serve.
- Make a mobile that demonstrates the diverse web of life in the ocean.

Zany Zones

Cast of Characters

Zooplankton 1	Octopus
Zooplankton 2	Sea Cucumber
Phytoplankton 1	Sea Star
Phytoplankton 2	Tube Worm
Jellyfish	Crab
Herring	Lobster
Whale	Clam 1
Giant Ray	Clam 2
Squid	Clam 3
Butterfly Fish	Snail

Optional Props
- Blue bed sheet to make waves
- Signs worn to identify sea creatures

Setting: Ocean

Zany Zones

Zooplankton 1: I know you keep telling me we are the most important animals in the ocean, but what good is that when nobody can see us?

Zooplankton 2: It doesn't matter that we are so tiny people can't see us. We are the most important link in the food web and get to live in the sunlight zone. We have privacy, not like those celebrity dolphins, and that's good.

Phytoplankton 1: I beg your pardon! Everyone knows that plant plankton, not animal plankton, is the basic food of the ocean. That makes us the most important link in the food web.

Phytoplankton 2: Don't pay any attention to them. They are always bragging. It makes them feel better about themselves. It's no fun being called "shrimp" all your life. Shrimp! (pause) See it hurts.

Jellyfish: I can't believe what I'm hearing! We are all part of the plankton classification. We are known as the floaters and drifters. Not a terribly distinguished description, if you want my opinion.

Herring: Come on, here come the drifters again.

Whale: Eat, eat, eat! That's all you ever do!

Herring: That is all I do? That's all you do, too!

Giant Ray: Do you have any idea how much plankton you guys have to eat to get one good meal? Why don't you eat fish like some of the other sea creatures in the nekton classification?

Zooplankton 2: Disgusting. I never eat anything with a face. I guess that makes me a vegan.

Squid: What's a vegan? More importantly, what's nekton? Does that include me?

Butterfly Fish: Yes, that includes you and all of the other animals that can swim freely in water without the help of currents. Most of us live in the upper zones of the ocean, but we can go to all of the zones.

Octopus: Look out! Here comes another member of the family! Shark! (make shark movie sound effect)

Sea Cucumber: Do you mind? You are stepping on me! Just look at me. I am less cucumber-ry now.

Sea Star: Oops! Sorry, old man. No disrespect meant. You just kind of blend in with the ocean floor.

Tube Worm: Many of the creatures that live on the bottom do. I'm an exception. I stand out and as you can see, I have a very striking color. It's okay, you can look. Take a picture if you like.

Crab: You think you're so great! You may be attractive, but what kind of protection do you have?

Lobster: Don't mind him, he's just crabby. Get it? Crabby! See, he's a crab and I said crabby. That's a pun!

Clam 1: We get it. It's just not that funny. Do you guys mind? We're trying to get some sleep down here.

Clam 2: We've had a terrible day! Divers collected several members of our family today!

Clam 3: It's tragic! We need you to give us a break and clam up! Hey Lobster, did you get that?

Snail: All of you benthos creatures better clam up. Here come more divers and a submersible.

Founders or Partners?

Pre-Reading Activities:

Vocabulary Development

Have students define founder. Have students compare that word with "partner".

Assessing Prior Knowledge

Ask students if they know the founders of their city, county, or country. Have them list as many as possible.

Ask students to explain their understanding of veterinary medicine and why they think it is important.

Post-Reading Activities:

Inferences

Ask: How do you think researchers in human medicine and surgical techniques could benefit from collaborating with researchers in veterinary medicine and vice versa?

Research

Challenge students to locate specific examples of how human and veterinary branches of medicine have benefited from each other in recent years.

Challenge students to discover founders or "fathers" or "mothers" in other fields or movements such as religion, civil rights, sports, music, art, etc. They should present the information in a creative format such as a song, mural, skit, or diorama.

Founders or Partners?

Cast of Characters

Aspyrtus: Serious and straight man

Vegetius: Funny without realizing it

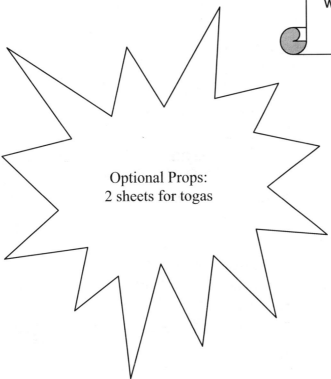

Optional Props:
2 sheets for togas

Aspyrtus: Greetings from the past, like over 2,000 years ago past. My name is Aspyrtus and I'm known as the Father of Veterinary Medicine.

Vegetius: So I guess that makes me the mother? Excuse me, I thought **we** were known as the **Founders** of Veterinary Medicine.

Aspyrtus: Well, it depends on what book you read. Oh how rude of me. Let me introduce my **partner**, from the Byzantine Empire, **Vegetius**. We worked together to write the first detailed guide for veterinarians. It was a best seller for many years.

Vegetius: (pointing to partner and saying with great pride) You see, Aspyrtus was the leading veterinarian of his day and personally described many of the medical and surgical problems associated with the horse and cow. I never was an actual veterinarian myself. I was just very good at writing down details, adding drawings, and expanding on the comments made by my esteemed colleague.

Aspyrtus: Yes, expanding on **my** comments (looks disgusted). Anyway, I think we are getting ahead of ourselves. I believe we are here to enlighten these youth on the history of veterinary medicine.

Vegetius: Very well. You begin and I will expand.

Aspyrtus: Wow, thanks! Before human beings were "civilized" they viewed animals, all animals, as a source of food and clothing. They even moved from place to place to follow them.

Vegetius: It was eat or be eaten!

Aspyrtus: Thank you… eventually, humankind began to stay in one place and grow crops. That is when they began domesticating animals. They discovered that some animals, such as horses and oxen, could help them with work.

Vegetius: They also discovered it was much easier to raise their own meat instead of chasing after it.

Aspyrtus: That's where veterinarians came in. People started realizing that they needed to keep their animals healthy.

Vegetius: Still, veterinarians didn't get a lot of respect or attention. Take Aspyrtus for example…he wasn't really appreciated until he was gone.

Aspyrtus: That's true. The medical profession was more concerned with its own growth than with the care of livestock.

Vegetius: It took some terrible plagues with millions of animals and humans dying before people took veterinary medicine seriously. I guess that's understandable.

Aspyrtus: That's when sick animals were finally isolated from healthy animals and keeping animals in clean environments took hold.

Vegetius: Medical doctors also saw how some diseases in animals could affect the health of humans and started working together.

Aspyrtus: Hurrah for veterinarians! (confetti falls down – victory dance!)

Vegetius: Thank you, Aspyrtus.

Aspyrtus: I meant ALL veterinarians.

Vegetius: Yes and thank you!

Penny For Your Thoughts. . .

Imagine the field of veterinary medicine had never been developed. What problems could have evolved from the absence of veterinary medicine?

Act 2

Adaptations

ADAPTATIONS

In literature, adaptations mean to change from its original form. Many movies that are popular today originated as novels, folk tales or even comic books.

When a piece of literature is changed or adapted to another form there are often positive and/or negative comparisons to the original.

The first example in this book, *The Bundle of Sticks*, is a fable told many years ago. There are a number of versions of this story and no one is absolutely certain what the original looked like. Although the language can be changed or adapted to the times, the moral for this tale is the same.

In the second example, *How Does It Feel To Live Next Door To a Giraffe* is made into a play directly from the text as written by the original author. Many changes can be made to increase or decrease the impact of the story.

Have students explain how this story can help illustrate a need for tolerance.

The third adaptation takes just the moral from the Tortoise and the Hare (slow and steady wins the race) and adapts the story to a more modern and relevant setting.

Have students compare and contrast this adaptation to the original version. After completion of this section of Reader's Theater, have students select a book, fairy tale or fable to adapt into a script. You may want to use the rubric at the back of the book to help guide students.

A Bundle of Sticks

Pre-Reading Activities:

Vocabulary Development
Have students define *fable*.

Have students define *moral* as it relates to fables and list as many morals as they can remember from reading.

Assessing Prior Knowledge
In a small group, have student brainstorm as many titles of fables that they can.

Post-Reading Activities:

Reading Comprehension
Have students repeat the moral of this fable, then rewrite in their own words.

Literary Response
Have students summarize or paraphrase this fable. Challenge them to write the gist of the fable in ten words or less.

Expressing Ideas in Writing
Allow students to work in small groups to write a play that teaches the same moral or lesson but is set in modern times. Have students assign parts then act out their plays for the class.

A Bundle of Sticks

Note to Teacher

This reader's theater is adapted from a fable credited to Aesop between 1909 and 1914.

Cast of Characters
Narrator 1
Narrator 2
Narrator 3
Son 1
Son 2
Son 3
Daughter 1
Daughter 2
Daughter 3
Father

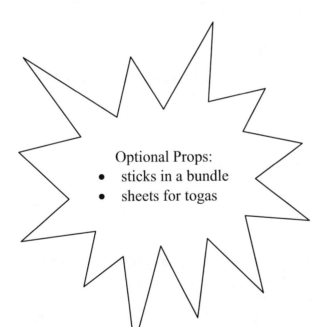

Optional Props:
- sticks in a bundle
- sheets for togas

Setting: a small hut in a village years ago

Narrator 1: A fable is a short lesson, told as a story, about how people behave. A moral at the end of each fable summarized the lesson of the story. Most fables use animals as characters. People have been telling fables for thousands of years. They are simple, wise, and funny. Through the years, humans have learned the same practical lessons that you and I are learning today.

Narrator 2: The person most associated with the fable is a man named Aesop. Aesop was a Greek slave. We don't know much about him, but some people think he would tell these stories in order to make a point in an argument. For almost 2,500 years, people have been telling the fables of Aesop.

Narrator 3: It is our pleasure to share with you a fable by Aesop. This fable is different from most because it uses human characters, not animals. It is called, "A Bundle of Sticks".

(Narrators exit. Sons and Daughters are arguing with each other on stage when the father enters the room.)

Father: Stop this racket! I cannot stand to listen to this constant arguing. You fight like cats and dogs. But even cats and dogs take a break once in a while.

Daughter 1: But Father, can I help it if everyone is in the kitchen at once trying to get breakfast? I'm the one who is supposed to cook the food, but I can't because he (points to Son 1.) won't bring me more wood. (holds up bundle of sticks)

Son 1: How can I bring more when there is no wood in the woodpile? He (points to Son 2) won't chop more wood.

Son 2: How can I chop more wood if my ax blade is dull. She (points to Daughter 2) is supposed to sharpen it.

Daughter 2: I would gladly sharpen the ax if she (points to Daughter 3) would return the grindstone she borrowed from me.

Daughter 3: How can I return a grindstone that I can't find because he (points to Son 3) lets the weeds grow behind the barn where the grindstone is kept.
Son 3: Weeds! Those aren't weeds! Those are vegetables I'm growing so that all of us can have fresh food.

(All sons and daughters began to argue again.)

Father: (raising voice) Stop! Stop! Stop! You will never get anything done if you do not cooperate. Let me show you. (picks up bundle of sticks and turns to Son 3) Here, break this bundle of sticks across your knee.

Son 3: (tries, but fails to break the bundle of sticks) I can't do it.

(Each son and daughter tries to break the bundle of sticks over his/her knee, saying, "I can't do it," and passing it to the next in line. The last in line passes the bundle back to the father.)

Father: There. Each of you tried to do it without the help of others and failed. I'm going to give you another chance. Take this (undo bundle and give one stick to each son and daughter) Now see if you can break the sticks.

(All sons and daughters break their sticks.)

Father: You see. When you work together, instead of putting the blame on one another, you can get the job done. Now, let's have some breakfast.

(Sons, daughters and father exit.)

Narrator 3: So the brothers and the sisters each learned that by taking responsibility for doing their tasks and working together, they were able to get the job done. When Son 3 went to his vegetable garden, he cleared the weeds and found the grindstone for Daughter 3, who promptly returned it to Daughter 2, who sharpened the ax for Son 2, who then chopped the wood for Son 1, who carried it in for Daughter 1, who gladly cooked a delicious breakfast for them all.

Narrator 2: The breakfast wasn't the best part of the fable.

Narrator 1: What was the best part of the fable?

(Everyone comes back on stage, holds hands and says…)

All: Learning that there is no strength like the strength found in teamwork.

Pre-Reading Activities:

Prediction
Have students discuss what a play entitled "How Does It Feel to Live Next Door to a Giraffe?" could be about.

Assessing Prior Knowledge
Explain that this play takes place in a zoo. Ask students to brainstorm the kinds of animals that might be found in a zoo and the special needs each of these animals would have.

Vocabulary Development
Have students define and share examples of tolerance.

Post-Reading Activities:

Reading Comprehension
Ask: What lesson do you think the author wanted you to get from reading this play? How could you apply this lesson in your life?

Research
Tell students zoos have changed during the past 200 years. Have them research these differences and make a visual display that illustrates the changes.

Expressing Ideas in Writing
Have students explain how they would redesign the zoo in this story to make conditions better for these animals. Challenge them to further explain whether they think it would solve the problems.

Have students write a dialogue between a grandfather gorilla and his grandchild about the way it was in the "good old days" before zoos were more attuned to conservation. Were the days really "good"?

How Does it Feel to Live Next Door to a Giraffe?

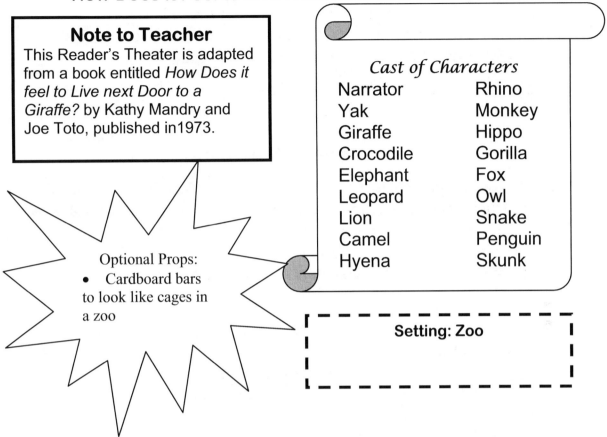

Note to Teacher
This Reader's Theater is adapted from a book entitled *How Does it feel to Live next Door to a Giraffe?* by Kathy Mandry and Joe Toto, published in1973.

Optional Props:
• Cardboard bars to look like cages in a zoo

Cast of Characters

Narrator	Rhino
Yak	Monkey
Giraffe	Hippo
Crocodile	Gorilla
Elephant	Fox
Leopard	Owl
Lion	Snake
Camel	Penguin
Hyena	Skunk

Setting: Zoo

Narrator: Everybody has a next door neighbor. You do and your friends do. Even the animals at the zoo have neighbors. They live very close to each other. Do you think you'd like that? How do you think the animals feel? Let's find out. Let's ask the giraffe how he feels about living next door to the yak.

Yak: The giraffe? Don't make me laugh. I call him The Neck. He's always sticking his big neck in here to steal my food. If I turn my head, my lunch is gone. If I take a little nap, there goes my dinner! I get skinnier and skinnier every day while The Neck gets fatter and fatter.

Giraffe: Don't listen to that yak. He pushes his fur into my cage. It makes me sneeze a lot. Don't think it's so easy for a giraffe to sneeze. A-ch-ch-ch-ch-oo-oo-oo! If I must have a neighbor, let it be the elephant. He has good manners.

Crocodile: Good manners! He blows peanut shells in my water all day. How would you like to swim in peanut shells? They get stuck in my teeth. Just look at this mess!

Elephant: That crocodile is not my idea of a good neighbor. He's always making waves and sneaking up on me. His teeth look funny to me, too. I think he should see a dentist. If I must have a neighbor, I'd like to live near the lion. He's the king of beasts.

Leopard: The lion? He sure doesn't seem like a king to me! He keeps telling me to go to a dry cleaner. He thinks I should have my spots removed. Well, he needs a haircut! That's not all. His roar makes my ears feel fuzzy (shakes head).

Lion: That leopard is too nervous. He paces back and forth in his cage. Back and forth. Back and forth. At least try forth and back for a change. How would you like to see moving spots in front of your eyes all day? To live next to him you need to wear a pair of sunglasses. If I must have a neighbor, give me one with a sense of humor. The hyena!

Camel: You want to live next door to laughing boy? Do you think you'd like to be laughed at all day? He even laughs at night in his sleep. If I'm sick, he laughs. If I yawn, he laughs. When I eat, he laughs. He even pokes fun at the way that I look. It's no fun to be laughed at all the time.

Hyena: Hee! Hee! Hee! I have low self-esteem. It's how I deal. That camel can't take a joke. He's too serious. Hee! Hee! All he talks about are the long hot days in the desert. Hee! Hee! And how long he can go without water. Hee! Hee! I want someone to laugh with and make me feel special. If I must have a neighbor, let it be the monkey. He'd be a lot of fun! Hee! Hee!

Rhinoceros: Fun! Do you know what he does for fun? He throws banana peels in my cage and watches me slip and fall. I guess I should consider myself lucky though. I talked to the guy that used to live here. I don't want to tell what he used to throw at him. It took a professional a week to clean it up.

Monkey: That rhinoceros is so clumsy! He's always banging into my cage. He makes everything shake so much that I fall out of my swing. I wish I had a big brother around. He'd take care of me. If I must have a neighbor, let it be the gorilla.

Hippopotamus: Some big brother! All he does is play in his rubber tire. He thinks he's smart because he can do things with his opposable thumbs. If he beats his chest one more time, I think I'll bellow!

Gorilla: That hippopotamus is an old mudball! He wallows in mud all day. He splashes it in my cage! Then he opens his big mouth and bellows at me. He sounds like a sick tuba. If I must have a neighbor, let it be the owl. He's smart.

Fox: I wanted someone I could talk to. But all the owl ever says is, "Whooo." If I ask him a question, he says, "Whooo." He even says "Whooo," all night long when nobody is listening. I've been trying to teach him to at least say, "Whom." That would be different.

Owl: You have to watch a fox. He's sneaky. Did you know that he raided henhouses as a youth? That's right! He has a record. And that's not all. He never stops talking. He's always bothering me with his foolish words. With a neighbor like that, I'm lucky to get in a, "Whooo," once in a while. If I must have a neighbor, let it be the penguin. Everything is black and white with him.

Rattlesnake: That penguin thinks he's so important because he's dressed in a tuxedo and he was in a movie. Mr. Hollywood. He walks with his nose in the air. Who wants to live near him? I'm more down to earth.

Penguin: I don't like that snake. I don't like any snake. He's always hissing and striking out at me. HISS. HISS. HISSSSS. He has beady eyes, too. I don't trust him. If I had my way, I wouldn't have a neighbor.

Skunk: I hear everybody complaining about their neighbors. I get very lonely living by myself. I'd like to live next door to someone – anyone at all. Hello. Anyone?

Penny For Your Thoughts

Imagine you had to live in the zoo on display for all to see. Write a narrative entitled, "A Day in the Life of Me". The setting is in a zoo cage. What are your feelings?

Tortoise and the Hare

Pre-Reading Activities:

Vocabulary Development
Have students define adaptation as it applies in literature.

Assessing Prior Knowledge
Ask students to retell then summarize the well known Aesop's Fable *The Tortoise and the Hare*. Have students discuss the moral or lesson illustrated in this fable.

Prediction
Tell students the lesson from this famous tale has been used in a modern day version with people instead of animals. Ask them to predict what the scenario might be.

Post-Reading Activities:

Compare and Contrast
Ask: How do you think this adaptation is the same and different when compared to *The Tortoise and the Hare*.

Expressing Ideas in Writing
Say: When thinking back on the play which student do you identify with most and explain why.

Tell students to imagine this story has just come out in a story collection book in the library and they were asked to write a critique for the school newspaper. Ask: How would you describe the story? Would you give it a thumbs-up or thumbs down? Why?

Research
Challenge students to go to the library and see how many adaptations they can find of some of their favorite fairy tales, folk tales, fables, and classics. Have students select one they like better than the original and share it with the class.

The Tortoise and the Hare

Note to Teacher

This is an adaptation of *The Tortoise and the Hare*. In Aesop's version of this famous fable the characters are all animals.

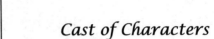

Cast of Characters

Teacher
Student 1
Student 2
Student 3
Student 4
Student 5

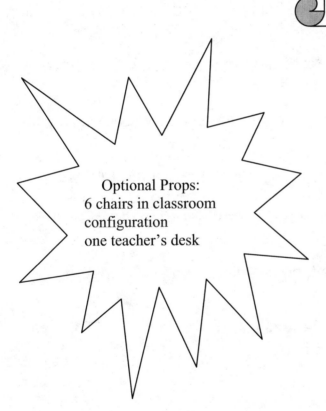

Optional Props:
6 chairs in classroom configuration
one teacher's desk

Setting: Students are seated in a classroom waiting for the teacher to arrive.

Student 1: I am going to finish this test so fast. I'm going to have it done before you can put your name on yours.

Student 2: We have a test?

Student 3: Yes we do. Every Friday and every Friday you forget.

Student 2: Well at least I remember to forget.

Student 4: (nervously) This test is life or death. If I don't pass I'll never be an astronaut.

Student 3: You have never earned less than an "A". You're the smartest person I have ever met and I've meet a lot of people.

Student 4: Thanks. All those good grades could have been a fluke, a mere flash in the pan, an oasis in the middle of a desert…

Student 1: Whatever! I'm going to finish first and be on the bus sitting by the window.

Student 5: So what if you get to sit next to the window. You have been in the same grade for two years.

Student 1: Yeah, but I always sit next to the window. Look at my tan. Just look at it.

Student 5: Well it is nice, don't get me wrong, even though everyone knows by now how damaging the sun's rays can be to the skin, I just think you should take your time, read carefully and think about the answer.

Student 2: Teacher! Hide! Wait, never mind, don't hide. We're supposed to be here.

Teacher: (entering the room) Okay class, we have a test. Take out your pencils and put away your things.

Student 2: (raises hand)

Teacher: Yes we have a test.

Student 2: (puts hand down)

Student 1: I'm going to finish first!

Teacher: Please take your time. I like you but having you in my class for two years in a row is enough. I think three years is pushing it.

Student 3: Can I pass out the tests?

Teacher: Yes, you may but no extra points.

Student 3: Well, I guess I'll still do it. (passes out the test)

Student 1: Finished! Done! Have a good day!

Teacher: Are you sure you're finished?

Student 1: Well of course. I'm the fastest. (hands teacher his test, starts to go)

Teacher: You don't have permission to leave. I've decided to let the person with the highest score go first today.

Student 1: What? No way! What about my tan and my perfect window sitting record. You have to let me go. (pleading)

Teacher: I'm sorry. You have to take your time and do things right the first time.

Student 2: We're all done.

Teacher: Thank you (teacher starts grading papers) All right you all got an "A" except one. (pointing at Student One) You got the worst score I have ever seen. You even got your name wrong.

Student 1: My record of sitting by the window. My perfect tan. (leaves the room hanging head and mumbling to himself)

Teacher: See you next year.

The moral to the story: Slow and steady wins the race.

Act 3

Format Models

Format Models

In the following section students will be introduced to a variety of formats they can use as models to create their own scripts.

In *Heeerrreee's Fossil* the script is patterned after a talk show interview. The guest in this example is an inanimate object, a fossil. The fossil takes on human characteristics (personification). Have students take on the persona of a talk show host and select a person or thing to interview. This will require research in order for the guest speaker to sound knowledgeable about his or her subject.

In *Time Travelers* have students imagine they are traveling in a time machine. Tell them they can set the date for their time machine to any event in history. They are to research the event then write a script as if they were actually witnessing the event as it unfolds. Before the class makes their presentations, have students build a time machine built for two using boxes, recyclables, plastic pipe, etc. and lots of imagination.

Examples three and four are modeled after a retro 1950s television game show entitled, "To Tell the Truth". Each of the three contestants claims to be the same person. The panelists (the rest of the class) have to determine which one of the three contestants is telling the truth. After researching an historic figure, have students create a script.

The last two models are examples of choral readings. The first is a narrative about a real period in history involving scientists when dinosaur bones were more rare and valuable than diamonds.

The second choral reading model is a fun example of pure fairy tale fiction. Have students select one of the two models and create their own choral reading.

Heeerrreee's Fossil

Cast of Characters

Talk Show Host (a loud and lively person that smiles a lot)

Fossil (appears very old and very stiff and very cranky)

Optional Props:
- 2 chairs facing audience
- microphone

Setting: on the stage of a game show

Talk Show Host (TSH): Hello, and welcome to our fabulous, one-of-a-kind talk show. Today we have a very special guest – a fossil. *(applause)*

Without further ado, let me introduce you to our guest. (applause, but nobody comes for a very long time; fossil is very old and moves quite slowly)

Are you there, Fossil?

Fossil: What's the rush? I'll be there! Hold your trilobites! (Fossil slowly, stiffly walks on stage.)

TSH: Welcome! (Both sit and turn to audience.) So, you're a fossil.

Fossil: Yep, That's what they call me.

TSH: What is a fossil?

Fossil: You invite me on your talk show and you don't even know what I am? You obviously didn't do your homework. I should have held out for Oprah!

TSH: Well, I do know that a fossil is a plant or an animal that was preserved in lime, mud, or sand and that turned into rock.

Fossil: Could be tar, ice, or tree sap, too.

TSH: Oh yes. I know that. I guess I just wasn't sure whether you're a plant or an animal fossil.

Fossil: Isn't it obvious?

TSH: No.

Fossil: I am an Echinoid. (i-ki'noid) Of or like a sea urchin.

TSH: *(saying sarcastically)* Well, that really clears things up. I understand some plants and animals become fossils naturally, but some are trapped into becoming fossils. Is that what happened to you?

Fossil: Yes, that did happen to me. I was walking along, minding my own business when – WHOOSH, mud from a river flood rushed over me. I was buried with all of the other plants and animals around me. It was horrible. *(starts to cry.)*

TSH: Why didn't you just crawl out of the mud?

Fossil: Easy for you to say. Do you have any idea how heavy sand and mud can be when piled layer upon layer? Besides, I'd skipped breakfast that day – the most important meal of the day – and was feeling a little weak. *(starts to cry, again)*

TSH: I'm sorry. I didn't know this would be so painful for you to relive.

Fossil: That's OK. I've only been a fossil for a few million years. I understand it gets easier.

TSH: If I may ask, how did you get so *(pauses to think of a nice way to say)* inflexible?

Fossil: Oh, that. The water helped the minerals stick together, and they locked up the sand particles to form a hard rock.

TSH: Wow! What happened next?

Fossil: I dissolved as the extra water was squeezed out. What you see before you is actually just the shape of what I used to be.

TSH: Are you petrified?

Fossil: No, I've been on television before. This is nothing.

TSH: No, what I mean by petrified is — do rock minerals fill in some parts of your body?

Fossil: Oh, that kind of petrified. No, I'm actually just a mold, but a really good one. (winks to audience)

TSH: Well, that's all we have time for today. Thank you for coming. You've been an… *interesting* guest. Please come back *(lowers voice)* in another millions years.

Fossil: You'll have to talk to my agent about that. *(applause as fossil walks off slowly)*

Penny For Your Thoughts. . .
The "guest" on the talk show is a thing from a long time ago. What if you were to write a script for a "guest" from our future? Who or what would the guest be and what information would be shared?

Cast of Characters

Time Traveler 1

Time Traveler 2

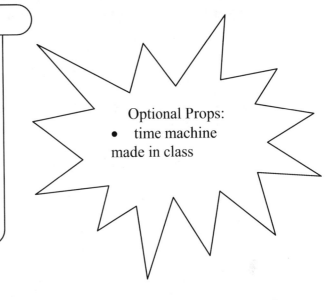

Optional Props:
- time machine made in class

Settings on Time Machine: Date: Sunday, April 9th, 1865, place: Appomattox, Virginia, event: End of the Civil War, Surrender

Time Traveler 1: Wow, what a beautiful farmhouse. You can tell there has been a war though – no crops and the house is in need of some repairs. I'll bet before the war it was a showplace.

Time Traveler 2: Look at all the soldiers. They look so tired and worried. I guess fighting for 4 years will age anyone.

TT1: I suppose so. It looks like the soldiers are evenly divided. The confederate soldiers, wearing gray, are on one side and the union soldiers, wearing dark blue, are on the other side.

TT2: Look, I see what appears to be two leaders, generals, coming forward.

TT1: Yes, there is General Robert E. Lee, he has on a spotless dress uniform complete with sword. He looks so distinguished. He must be very sad today.

TT2: It must be hard to surrender to your enemy after such a hard struggle.

TT1: Here comes General Ulysses S. Grant. His uniform is mud-spattered and he's just wearing a private's coat with general's stripes. I wonder why?

TT2: Maybe he didn't want to look like he was gloating or bragging about the victory.

TT1: Look, they are shaking hands now.

TT2: Now they are sitting down with a piece of important looking paper.

TT1: I'll bet that is the surrender agreement.

TT2: Yes, every time there is a war, at the end many important decisions have to be made.

TT1: Can you get a closer look at the paper?

TT2: Sure, let me use my laser advancing magnifier adjustment here.

TT1: That's great! I can read it perfectly now. It says that all of the prisoners from war will be given food and released at once. The southern soldiers can even keep their horses and weapons.

TT2: That sounds fair. You know that during the war almost 600,000 people died and the cost of the war totaled nearly $15 billion.

TT1: What a waste! Look, the generals are standing up again. They are shaking hands and bowing to each other. What an exciting event in our history!

TT2: I guess we know what happens next.

TT1: You mean that the south rejoined the north and we remain the United States of America to this very day?

TT2: No, we go back to the real world and become students again.

TT1: Oh yeah, well…buckle up!

TT2: Here we go!

To Tell the Truth

Cast of Characters

Narrator or Teacher
Game Show Host
George Washington Carver 1
George Washington Carver 2
George Washington Carver 3

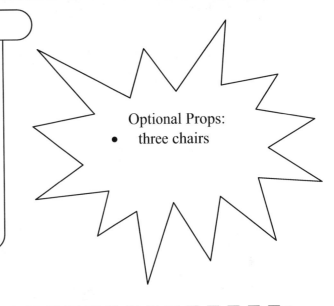

Optional Props:
- three chairs

Setting: on a game show

Narrator or Teacher: Today we are going to play a game called "To Tell The Truth". Each of three contestants will claim to be the same person, in this case, George Washington Carver. The panelists (that's all of you) will guess which one of the three contestants is telling the truth. Take a minute now to write the numbers 1 to 8. When I read a question listen carefully to the answers from the three contestants. The phony claimants could lie or exaggerate the truth but the "real" George Washington Carver has "to tell the truth" when questioned. At the conclusion of the show, I will say, "Will the real George Washington Carver please stand up or step forward." And you will see if you were correct.

Game Show Host: Hello contestants. Will you please identify yourselves.

George Washington Carver #1: I am George Washington Carver.

George Washington Carver #2: I am George Washington Carver.

George Washington Carver #3: I am George Washington Carver.

Game Show Host: (speaking to audience) Obviously all three of these contestants cannot be George Washington Carver. It is your job to listen carefully to the answers each one gives to the questions that I pose. The "real" George Washington Carver will always tell the truth. You are welcome to take notes during the questioning so you can eliminate the imposters by the end of the game.

Question number 1: When were you born?

GWC#1: I was born October 10, 1859, right when the Civil War was starting up.

GWC#2: I was born some time during the Civil War years. Birth records of slaves were not very accurate.

GWC#3: I was born near the end of the Civil War, just as freedom was declared.

Question number 2: How did you manage to get such a good education?

GWC#1: The family that owned my mother adopted me after her death. They made sure I was well educated.

GWC#2: I learned everything I could from everybody I came in contact with. I would move from place to place in search of more knowledge. I earned my keep by taking in wash and doing odd jobs.

GWC#3: The family that owned my mother gave me land to farm. I educated myself until I saved enough money to go to college.

Question number 3: What type of scientist are you?

GWC#1: I am a botanist. I know everything there is to know about plants and their environment.

GWC#2: I work in the field of chemurgy. That is the science of developing industrial application of farm products.

GWC#3: I am strictly a research scientist. I develop formulas to help crops grow better and yield more.

Question number 4: What major award did you receive?

GWC#1: I was presented the Nobel Peace Prize in 1938 for my work to feed the hungry in the south.

GWC#2: I received the Spingarn Medal in 1923. The Spingarn Medal is awarded to the black person who has made the greatest contribution to the advancement of his or her race.

GWC#3: President Franklin Roosevelt named a national park after me in 1958 near my childhood home of Diamond Grove, Missouri. The park also has a statue of me.

Question number 5: Can you tell us some of the synthetic products you developed?

GWC#1: I developed eggbeaters, an egg substitute, plastic, and tile.

GWC#2: I developed Worcestershire Sauce, Vanishing Cream, and Cheese.

GWC#3: I developed cat litter, baby powder, and beef stew.

Question number 6: Is there anything about you that most people don't know or overlook?

GWC#1: Yes, I am the author of several books of poetry.

GWC#2: Yes, I am a musician and painter in addition to being a scientist.

GWC#3: Yes, I am an accomplished actor and singer.

Question number 7: What are you most proud of?

GWC#1: I developed 325 products from a sweet potato.

GWC#2: I left the world a better place than when I found it.

GWC#3: I received an honorary doctorate from Simpson College in 1928 and was made a member of the Royal Society of Arts in London, England.

Question number 8: What are you most famous for?

GWC#1: I believe I am most famous for my work with bees and honey and pollination.

GWC#2: I believe I am most famous for my work with sweet potatoes and peanuts.

GWC#3: I am most remembered for my development of a rubber substitute and over 500 dyes and pigments from 28 different plants.

Game Show Host: (speaking to audience) Take a few minutes to decide who you think is the "real" George Washington Carver. Is it George Washington Carver #1, George Washington Carver #2, or George Washington Carver #3? (have students write their selection on a note card or journal)

Game Show Host: Will the real George Washington Carver please stand up. (or step forward; after a little teasing George Washington Carver #2 stands up)

NOTE: Have students discuss clues that helped them make the correct choice. Review the answers from the GWC #2 Contestant so there are no misunderstandings.

Penny For Your Thoughts. . .
Think about all the contributions George Washington Carver #2 shared during the reader's theater. What do you think is the most impressive contribution and why?

To Tell the Truth

Ancient Nubian Royalty

Cast of Characters

Narrator or Teacher
Game Show Host
Nubian Royalty #1
Nubian Royalty #2
Nubian Royalty #3

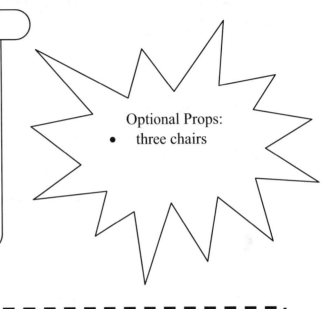

Optional Props:
- three chairs

Setting: on a game show

Narrator or Teacher: Today we are going to play a game called "To Tell The Truth." Each of three contestants will claim to be real ancient Nubian royalty. The panelists (that's all of you) will guess which one of the three contestants is telling the truth. Take a minute now to write the numbers 1 to 5. When I read a question listen carefully to the answers from the three contestants. The phony claimants could lie or exaggerate the truth but the "real" Nubian royalty has "to tell the truth" when questioned. At the conclusion of the show, I will say, "Will the real Nubian royalty please stand up or step forward." And you will see if you were correct.

Game Show Host: Hello contestants. Will you please identify yourselves.

NR#1: I am Nubian royalty.

NR #2: I am Nubian royalty.

NR #3: I am Nubian royalty.

Game Show Host: (speaking to audience) All three of these contestants are not Nubian royalty. It is your job to listen carefully to the answers each one gives to the questions that I pose. The "real" Nubian royalty will always tell the truth. You are welcome to take notes during the questioning so you can eliminate the imposters by the end of the game.

Question Number 1: Did you get involved in many wars?

NR 1: Yes, we often fought the Egyptians. I loved winning!

NR 2: Yes, but we only fought when we had to protect our territory.

NR 3: No, we only fought the Egyptians twice.

Question Number 2: What were some of the items you used to trade?

NR 1: We traded fur mostly but also bird and alligator eggs.

NR 2: We traded gold, ivory and beautiful ostrich feathers.

NR 3: We traded jewelry, metal pots, and fish.

Question Number 3: What items did you like to trade for?

NR 1: I liked to trade for fine leather boots and coats.

NR 2: I liked jewelry, metal pots, and Greek wine.

NR 3: I liked to trade for gold. You just can't have enough gold, you know!

Question Number 4: How were you buried?

NR 1: I was buried in a mound of earth with my favorite servants.

NR 2: I was buried in a pyramid made of sandstone. All of my body organs were in little jars.

NR 3: I was buried with all of my pets in a pyramid made of mudbrick.

Question number 5: What did you believe in?

NR 1: We only worshipped the sun god.

NR 2: We believed in many gods. Some were spirits and others were local gods such as the war god.

NR 3: We just believed in ourselves. We were the greatest!

Game Show Host: (speaking to audience) Take a few minutes to decide who you think is the "real" Nubian royalty. Is it #1, #2, or #3? (Have students write their selection on a note card or journal.)

Game Show Host: Will the real Nubian royalty please stand up (or step forward; after a little teasing #2 stands up)

NOTE: Have students discuss clues that helped them make the correct choice. Review the answers from Contestant #2 so there are no misunderstandings.

Huntin' Bones

Cast of Characters

Chorus: all students
Speakers 1 - 18

Optional Props:
pictures of bones

Setting: on a stage telling about fossils and bones

Chorus: Bones, bones, bones. Huntin' them bones, bones, bones.
Bones, bones, bones. Huntin' them bones, bones, bones.

Speaker 1:
Fossils are remains of animals from long ago.
The story we tell today is of hunters that we know.

Chorus

Speaker 2:
Did you know that Thomas Jefferson hunted fossils just for fun?
He got Americans interested in hunting for some.

Chorus

Speaker 3:
Sir Richard Owen of England was looking for a name.
He discovered that "dinosaur" and "fearfully great" were the same.

Chorus

Speaker 4:
May Ann Mantell knew she'd found a tooth.
But wasn't sure how old it was.
She couldn't believe the truth!

Chorus

Speaker 5:
Her husband was a scientist who helped her with this unknown.
They found that the tooth belonged to the huge Iguanodon.

Chorus

Speaker 6:
There were two famous hunters that we ought to mention.
They turned the world of fossil hunting into a bone convention!

Chorus

Speaker 7:
You see, Othniel Marsh and Edward Cope were once very good friends.
But huntin' them old dinosaur bones soon made their friendship end.

Chorus

Speaker 8:
Mr. Marsh wanted to keep those bones for himself.
But Mr. Cope decided to put them on his shelf.

Chorus

Speaker 9:
Wherever Mr. Marsh would hunt Mr. Cope would be close by.
And wherever Mr. Cope would dig Mr. Marsh was there to spy!

Chorus

Speaker 10:
As the feud went on between them, they seemed to count the scores.
It got so bad that people called this feud the "Dinosaur Wars"!

Chorus

Speaker 11:
There was another hunter by the name of Barnum Brown.
People claimed he hunted by sniffing the ground.

Chorus

Speaker 12:
Barnum found some bones that made him quite perplexed.
The bones he found turned out to be the Tyrannosaurus rex!

Chorus

Speaker 13:
Barnum hunted dinosaur bones until he no longer would.
It is said that he discovered more bones than anyone could.

Chorus

Speaker 14:
There's one more dino hunter whose story we should tell.
His name is Roy Andrews. And he knew dinos well.

Chorus

Speaker 15:
He traveled to the Gobi Desert because of stories he'd heard.
I think he thought he'd find a prehistoric bird!

Chorus

Speaker 16:
He discovered a great treasure he never could have planned.
It was a nest of dino eggs that were buried in the sand.

Chorus

Speaker 17:
Andrews also found another dino kind of creature.
It was the very small, but fierce velociraptor.

Chorus

Speaker 18:
I think that I would like to be a dino hunter, too.
I wouldn't be greedy, just would like to find a few!

Chorus

The Emperor With a Rotten Attitude

Have students form five groups. Each group responds with the appropriate words and expressions when their cue (the character's name) is given in the reading of the story. Read through the story once so students can get familiar with their cues. All students will supply the sound effects of coughing and galloping horses at the end.

Characters	Response
The Emperor with a Rotten Attitude	hold nose and say, "P U"
Prince Who Dropped Out of School	shrug shoulders and say, "Whadja say?"
Prince Who is Muscle-Bound	make body poses and say, "G-r-r-r"
Prince Who is Kind, Intelligent, and Sensitive	smile broadly and bow, say "How Do You Do?"
Princess Who is Independent, Intelligent, and Clean with Great Teeth	curtsy and say, "Fine, Thank You, and You?"

Narrator 1:
There was once an emperor with a rotten attitude (**P U**). He had three sons. The eldest son dropped out of school (**Whadja Say?**)

The second son was exceedingly muscular; all he ever did was lift weights, pose and look at himself in the mirror (**G-r-r-r**).

The youngest son was kind, intelligent, and sensitive (**How Do You Do?**)

Narrator 2:
Now in nearby Indus Valley there lived an independent, intelligent, and clean princess with great teeth (**Fine, Thank you, and You?**) From birth she was told that there was an agreement written in

Sanskrit that she would marry one of the emperor's sons so their two powerful families could unite.

One day she came to the palace of the emperor with a rotten attitude (**P U**). "I have come," said she, "to seek a husband among your three sons." (**Whadja Say?, Gr-r-r-, and How do you do?**)

Narrator 3:

First she was introduced to the eldest son (**Whadja Say?**). She tried to carry on an intelligent conversation with him about current events, but every time she would ask for his opinion he would say (**Whadja Say?**).

Narrator 4:

Then the muscle-bound prince appeared (**Gr-r-r**), but every time she tried to bring up an interesting topic for discussion, he would just pose and say (**Gr-r-r-**).

Narrator 5:

The princess (**Fine thank you, and you?**) said to the emperor (**P U**), "These men will not make good husbands. What about your youngest son? (**How do you do?**)

This angered the emperor with a rotten attitude (**P U**). He said, "You cannot take my youngest son! (**How do you do?**)

Narrator 6:

"Well," she replied, "I cannot love your eldest son (**Whadja Say?**), and I don't like your muscle-bound son." (**Gr-r-r**)

Just then on the stairway appeared the youngest son (**How do you do?**) bowing courteously as he gazed upon the great teeth of the princess. The princess immediately struck up a conversation with him so they could get to know each other. The youngest son (**How do you do?**) appeared to be kind, intelligent, and sensitive to the feelings of the princess. (**Fine, thank you, and you?**)

Narrator 7:

Looking relieved, the princess announced, "I will take your youngest son (**How do you do?**) to be my husband so the agreement between our two families can be fulfilled."

Her words angered the emperor with a rotten attitude (**P U**). He wanted to keep his commitment to the princess's family and knew the union would be good for his empire, but he also knew his youngest son (**How do you do?**) was the only one of his three sons who had any sense.

Narrator 8:
"Call out the guards," he thundered, "and turn out this picky princess!" (**Fine, thank you, and you?**)

But the princess (**Fine, thank you and you?**) immediately grabbed the hand of the willing prince, (**How do you do?**) and rushed out the door. They both leaped upon her swift stallion and galloped off raising dust along the way. (**coughing and galloping sounds, which gradually fade away**)

Narrator 9:
The prince (**How do you do?**) and the princess (**Fine, thank you, and you?**) escaped safely because her army of equally intelligent, independent and clean ladies with great teeth stopped the emperor's men from following them. They did this, not by violence, but with engaging, interesting, and charming conversation.

Narrator 10:
So ends the romantic tale of the emperor with the rotten attitude (**P U**), his son who dropped out of school (**Whadja say?**), his muscle-bound son who posed all of the time, lifted weights and stared at himself in the mirror (**Gr-r-r**), and the youngest son who was kind, intelligent, and sensitive (**How do you do?**), and the independent, intelligent, and clean princess with great teeth (**Fine, thank you, and you?**) who had a fast-moving horse.

> **Penny For Your Thoughts. . .**
> Imagine you have been challenged to incorporate another prince into this play. Create his description and the phrase that would be mentioned each time the reader hears his name.

Act 4

Starters

Starters

The next two Reader's Theaters are incomplete. We got you started, but students need to do some research in order to complete the scripts.

First, have students work in small groups of five or six and read the script as it is written.

Next, have students use the furnished independent research sheets to gather enough information and facts so each group or student can add to the play.

Third, challenge students to find a place where they can insert their scripts. Make sure it flows and sounds connected. This may require changing the line that comes right before and right after.

Fourth, encourage students to practice the play and make any necessary changes within their small groups.

Finally, have students present the finished product to the class.

Cast of Characters

Roly-Poly Pillbug
(Narrator)
Rattlesnake
Lion
Other animals

Setting: Animal Defense
Convention

Roly-Poly Bug: I'm so excited! I'm finally here. The first Animal Defense Convention. This is my big chance. I can find out about all of the ways other animals protect themselves against predators, especially man.

Rattlesnake: Hi Roly! (laughs)

Roly-Poly Bug: Hi, Rattlesnake! What are you doing here? You already have great protection. (sounding envious)

Rattlesnake: I know, the greatest set of defenses, in my opinion. I can hear people coming by listening to the vibrations my jawbone sends to my inner ear. I can strike quickly or make scary noises. I have great camouflage, and don't forget my fearsome fangs and venom.

Roly-Poly Bug: Then, why are you here?

Rattlesnake: I guess you could call me a role model. I also like to show off and help other animals pick out or change their survival equipment or defense "tricks".

Roly-Poly Bug: Well, can you help me? How would I look with fangs? What about a rattle?

Rattlesnake: No, I don't think fangs and rattles are for you. I have to go now, the convention is beginning. Why don't you ask some other animals at the convention how they survive. Maybe some other kind of protection will suit you.

Roly-Poly Bug: (coming up to a group of animals…clearing throat) Excuse me! May I ask how you defend yourself?

Animal 1:

Animal 2:

Animal 3:

Animal 4:

Animal 5:

Animal 6:

Animal 7:

Roly-Poly Bug: These sound very interesting but so far I don't think any of these kinds of defenses are for me. I'd better ask some other animals what they do. (rolling up to another group of animals) Excuse me, what do you have for defense?

Animal 8:

Animal 9:

Animal 10:

Animal 11:

(more or fewer animals as needed for everyone to have a part)

Same convention 2 days later

Lion: Well, little buddy, the convention is almost over. Have you made a decision yet?

Roly-Poly Bug: Yes, I've decided to go with poison that I spit from my legs. Then I'm going to add spikes all over my body so that I inflict pain when anybody tries to touch me. I'm going to let out an incredible screeching sound that pierces through the air and stuns anyone within 2 miles if they come anywhere near me. What do you think?

Lion: Is that ALL? (speaking sarcastically but with a grin)

Roly-Poly Bug: Yeah! I think that will about do it. I guess I'll go now and put in my order.

BOOMING ANNOUNCEMENT: The convention is now officially over. Thank you for coming. Have a SAFE trip home. (DOOR SLAMS SHUT.)

Roly-Poly Bug: (sobbing) No! No! No! You can't mean it! Not over! Please let me in! It's a matter of life or death I'll only be a minute!

Lion: Don't worry, little buddy, there's always next year. In the meantime, just roll up in a really tight ball whenever you get scared. (Lion snickers and walks away.)

Roly-Poly Bug: Well you can laugh now, but wait until next year. Just wait until you see me then. I'll be big and bad! (rolls off)

Animal Defense
Independent Research

Select an animal and research what the animal uses for defense against predators. Use the following research form:

Animal:

_____

Method to Defend Against Predators:

_____

_____

_____

The Defense Works this way:_____

_____

_____

Script to be inserted in the Reader's Theater:

_____

_____

_____

Where should the script be inserted and how does it connect to the flow of the play?

_____

Cast of Characters

Teacher
Super Nut Man
Veggie Breath
additional characters as
inserted

Optional Props
Color transparency
or poster of the
newest food pyramid

Setting: Classroom

Teacher: Today we are fortunate to have Super Nut Man and his side kick Veggie Breath with us to introduce our next unit of study.

Super Nut Man: (acting insulted) Excuse me…that is pronounced Super Newt Man like the word <u>Nu</u>-trition. Not nut like an peanut.

Teacher: Oh excuse me. Can I just call you Newt then?

Super Nut Man: No, you can call me Super.

Teacher: Okay…Super…Would you like to start by explaining to the class why you and Veggie Breath are here.

Super Nut Man: Yes I will. Breath and I are alarmed at what we read in the papers and see on the news these days about the poor eating habits of Americans…adults and children.

Veggie Breath: Not only what they eat but how much they eat and how inactive they are!

Super Nut Man: I am here to explain the food pyramid and I'm sure I'll make it clear as mud.

Teacher: Don't you mean crystal clear?

Super Nut Man: (looks startled) Yes, of course I mean that. Please don't interrupt, I might get startled and accidentally run away. I have lightning reflexes you know.

Veggie Breath: (speaking very close to Super) Did you get your lightning reflexes from following the food pyramid?

Super Nut Man: Why yes. (covering nose) Please never talk to me that close again. I sure wish your brother fruit breath hadn't retired.

Teacher: Can we get back to the food pyramid?

Super Nut Man: Yes, I would but I must eat a piece off low fat cheese right now because my blood sugar is low. You take it Breath.

Veggie Breath: Okay! As you can see there are six columns, all different colors (show color transparency or poster of newest food pyramid). These colors represent the five different food groups plus oil.

Super Nut Man: Oil? I'm not drinking motor oil. That's disgusting! Is that why your breath is so bad?

Veggie Breath: Not motor oil, food oil. Like oil found in olives, fish, and **nuts**. My breath is bad because I need **two** AA batteries for my toothbrush and all I have is **one**.

Super Nut Man: Why are some stripes wider than others? (pause) Obviously I already know I'm just testing you.

Veggie Breath: The different sizes help remind you to choose more foods from certain groups and less from others. You should do this every day.

Students insert their scripts here about various healthy foods. They can write a script using Veggie Breath, Super Nut, the Teacher or add additional characters such as foods speaking for themselves or students responding to one of the characters in the play.

Veggie Breath: You should also do something active every day too.

Super Nut Man: Active, I've got you there. I skateboard with Tony Hawk every day.

Veggie Breath: You know Tony Hawk?

Super Nut Man: Yes he lives in a little box in my living room plugged into the T.V., I have no idea how he fits in there.

Veggie Breath: Playing a video game does not count as being active. Go running, walking, play outside, swim, bike or walk up stairs instead of using elevators.

Super Nut Man: I might just do all that today but not the elevator thing. I really love elevators.

Veggie Breath: You don't need to change overnight. Just start with one good thing and go from there.

Super Nut Man: (to the class) Well I hope I was able to make the food pyramid clear.

Teacher: Well class let's give Veggie Breath and his side kick Super Nut a big round of applause.

Super Nut Man: No Veggie Breath is **my** sidekick. You're funny!

Teacher: I was not trying to be funny.

Super Nut Man: My work here is done. Veggie Breath. Let's ride or walk, run, skip, or maybe you can carry me.

Veggie Breath: I'm not carrying you again. (Both exit)

Nutrition
Independent Research

Select a healthy food to research. What are the health benefits to eating this food? What is the portion size and how should it be cooked or served? Use the following research form:

Food:

_____

Health Benefit:

_____

_____

Portion size of this food:_____

_____

Way it should be cooked or served:_____

_____

_____

Script to be inserted in the Reader's Theater:

_____

_____

_____

Where should the script be inserted and how does it connect to the flow of the play?

_____

Reader's Theater Rubric

Partners: _____

Topic or Title: _____

Instructions: Mark the appropriate rating for each criterion. Use these individual ratings to assign an overall rating for the assignment.

Criteria	0 Working on It!	1 Novice	2 Acceptable	3 Out of the Box!
Uses Pre-Writing Strategies	Cannot generate pre-writing graphic organizers, notes, or brain-storming	Some use of pre-writing in the form of organizers, notes, or brainstorming	Use of more than one pre-writing strategy; mostly well-organized and thought-out	Numerous strategies used and followed to create a well-organized and thought-out composition
Content Is Valid and Accurate	Content is shallow and shows no insight	Content is accurate but lacks insight; few supporting examples	Content is accurate with some questions left unanswered and a few supporting examples	Content is 100 percent accurate and has supporting examples
Creativity	Could not express or present information	Presentation lacked creativity	Presentation moderately creative, entertaining, and informative	Engaging presentation that was creative, entertaining, and informative

Comments:

Blank Rubric

Student or Team: _____

Topic or Title: _____

Directions: Mark the appropriate rating for each criterion. Use these individual ratings to assign an overall rating for the assignment.

RATINGS	0 Working on it!	1 Novice	2 Acceptable	3 Out of the Box!	Not Applicable

Comments: